50 Canadian Dessert Recipes for Home

By: Kelly Johnson

Table of Contents

- Nanaimo Bars
- Butter Tarts
- Saskatoon Berry Pie
- BeaverTails
- Maple Syrup Pie
- Blueberry Grunt
- Flapper Pie
- Maple Fudge
- Date Squares
- Pouding Chômeur
- Apple Crisp
- Maple Butter Tart Squares
- Snow Taffy
- Caramelized Maple Apple Tart
- Maple Walnut Ice Cream
- Persimmon Pudding
- Rhubarb Crisp
- Blueberry Buckle
- Maple Shortbread Cookies
- Pumpkin Pie
- Maple Cake
- Bannock
- Maple Cream Pie
- Raspberry Fool
- Lemon Lush
- Baked Alaska
- Figgy Duff
- Maple Pecan Squares
- Sour Cream Pound Cake
- Canadian Sugar Pie
- Black Forest Cake
- Plum Pudding
- Maple Pecan Pie
- Butter Pecan Ice Cream
- Maple Oatmeal Cookies

- Raspberry Pie
- Maple Glazed Donuts
- Saskatoon Berry Crisp
- Wild Blueberry Pie
- Carrot Cake
- Pecan Pie
- Strawberry Rhubarb Pie
- Maple Brownies
- Butter Cake
- Peach Cobbler
- Maple Mousse
- Maple Bacon Donuts
- Gingerbread Cake
- Caramel Apple Pie
- Maple Custard

Nanaimo Bars

Ingredients

Base Layer:

- 1/2 cup unsalted butter
- 1/4 cup granulated sugar
- 5 tablespoons unsweetened cocoa powder
- 1 large egg, beaten
- 1 teaspoon vanilla extract
- 2 cups graham cracker crumbs
- 1 cup sweetened shredded coconut
- 1/2 cup chopped walnuts (optional)

Middle Layer:

- 1/2 cup unsalted butter, softened
- 2 cups powdered sugar
- 2 tablespoons vanilla custard powder (or instant vanilla pudding mix)
- 2-3 tablespoons milk

Top Layer:

- 4 ounces semi-sweet chocolate, chopped
- 2 tablespoons unsalted butter

Instructions

1. Prepare the Base Layer:
   - In a saucepan over low heat, melt the butter. Stir in the sugar and cocoa powder until well combined.
   - Add the beaten egg gradually, stirring constantly to prevent it from cooking.
   - Remove from heat and stir in the vanilla extract, graham cracker crumbs, shredded coconut, and walnuts (if using).
   - Press the mixture firmly into the bottom of an ungreased 8x8-inch baking pan. Refrigerate while preparing the middle layer.
2. Prepare the Middle Layer:
   - In a mixing bowl, cream together the softened butter, powdered sugar, and custard powder until smooth.

- Add the milk one tablespoon at a time, beating until the mixture is light and fluffy.
- Spread the middle layer evenly over the chilled base layer. Return to the refrigerator to set.
3. Prepare the Top Layer:
    - Melt the chopped chocolate and butter together in a heatproof bowl over a pot of simmering water (double boiler method) or in the microwave in short intervals, stirring until smooth.
    - Let the chocolate mixture cool slightly, then pour it over the chilled middle layer, spreading it evenly.
    - Chill in the refrigerator until the chocolate layer is set.
4. Serve:
    - Once set, remove from the refrigerator and allow to sit at room temperature for a few minutes before cutting into squares.
    - Use a sharp knife to cut the bars, wiping the knife clean between cuts to maintain neat edges.

Enjoy your homemade Nanaimo Bars! They can be stored in an airtight container in the refrigerator for up to a week, or frozen for longer storage.

Butter Tarts

Ingredients

Pastry:

- 1 1/4 cups all-purpose flour
- 1/4 teaspoon salt
- 1/2 cup unsalted butter, cold and cubed
- 1 large egg yolk
- 1 teaspoon vinegar
- Ice water

Filling:

- 1/2 cup unsalted butter, softened
- 1 cup brown sugar, packed
- 2 large eggs
- 1 teaspoon vanilla extract
- 1 tablespoon vinegar
- 1/4 cup light corn syrup or maple syrup
- 1/2 cup raisins or chopped pecans (optional)

Instructions

1. Prepare the Pastry:
    - In a large bowl, whisk together the flour and salt.
    - Add the cold, cubed butter. Use a pastry cutter or your fingers to cut the butter into the flour until the mixture resembles coarse crumbs.
    - In a small bowl, whisk together the egg yolk, vinegar, and enough ice water to make 1/4 cup of liquid.
    - Gradually add the liquid to the flour mixture, stirring with a fork until the dough comes together. If necessary, add a bit more ice water, a teaspoon at a time.
    - Form the dough into a disk, wrap in plastic wrap, and refrigerate for at least 30 minutes.
2. Prepare the Filling:
    - In a medium bowl, cream together the softened butter and brown sugar until light and fluffy.

- Beat in the eggs, one at a time, then add the vanilla extract, vinegar, and corn syrup (or maple syrup), mixing until well combined.
- If using, stir in the raisins or chopped pecans.

3. Assemble the Tarts:
    - Preheat the oven to 375°F (190°C).
    - On a lightly floured surface, roll out the chilled dough to about 1/8 inch thick. Cut out 4-inch circles using a cookie cutter or the rim of a glass.
    - Gently fit the circles into a standard muffin tin, pressing them into the bottom and up the sides.
    - Fill each pastry shell about two-thirds full with the prepared filling.
4. Bake:
    - Bake in the preheated oven for 15-20 minutes, or until the filling is bubbly and the pastry is golden brown.
    - Let the tarts cool in the pan for about 10 minutes, then carefully remove them and transfer to a wire rack to cool completely.

Enjoy your homemade Butter Tarts! They can be stored in an airtight container at room temperature for a few days or refrigerated for longer storage.

Saskatoon Berry Pie

Ingredients

Pie Crust:

- 2 1/2 cups all-purpose flour
- 1 teaspoon salt
- 1 cup unsalted butter, cold and cubed
- 1/4 to 1/2 cup ice water

Filling:

- 5 cups fresh or frozen Saskatoon berries
- 1 cup granulated sugar
- 3 tablespoons cornstarch
- 1/4 teaspoon salt
- 1 tablespoon lemon juice
- 1/4 teaspoon almond extract (optional)
- 2 tablespoons butter, cut into small pieces

Egg Wash (optional):

- 1 egg, beaten
- 1 tablespoon water

Instructions

1. Prepare the Pie Crust:
    - In a large bowl, whisk together the flour and salt.
    - Add the cold, cubed butter. Use a pastry cutter or your fingers to cut the butter into the flour until the mixture resembles coarse crumbs.
    - Gradually add the ice water, a tablespoon at a time, mixing with a fork until the dough begins to come together. Add just enough water for the dough to hold together without being sticky.
    - Divide the dough in half, shape each half into a disk, wrap in plastic wrap, and refrigerate for at least 30 minutes.
2. Prepare the Filling:
    - In a large bowl, combine the Saskatoon berries, sugar, cornstarch, and salt. Toss to coat the berries evenly.

- Add the lemon juice and almond extract (if using), and gently mix to combine.
3. **Assemble the Pie:**
    - Preheat the oven to 425°F (220°C).
    - On a lightly floured surface, roll out one disk of dough to fit a 9-inch pie plate, leaving some overhang. Fit the dough into the pie plate.
    - Pour the berry mixture into the pie crust and dot with the small pieces of butter.
    - Roll out the second disk of dough and place it over the filling. Trim and crimp the edges to seal, and cut a few small slits in the top crust to allow steam to escape.
    - If desired, brush the top crust with the egg wash made by beating the egg with water. This will give the crust a glossy finish.
4. **Bake:**
    - Bake the pie at 425°F (220°C) for 15 minutes.
    - Reduce the oven temperature to 350°F (175°C) and continue baking for 35-45 minutes, or until the crust is golden brown and the filling is bubbly.
    - If the edges of the crust start to brown too quickly, cover them with aluminum foil.
5. **Cool:**
    - Let the pie cool on a wire rack before serving to allow the filling to set.

Enjoy your homemade Saskatoon Berry Pie! It can be served warm or at room temperature, often with a scoop of vanilla ice cream or a dollop of whipped cream.

BeaverTails

Ingredients

Dough:

- 1/2 cup warm water (110°F or 45°C)
- 5 teaspoons active dry yeast
- 1 pinch granulated sugar
- 1 cup warm milk (110°F or 45°C)
- 1/3 cup granulated sugar
- 1 1/2 teaspoons salt
- 1 teaspoon vanilla extract
- 2 large eggs
- 1/3 cup vegetable oil
- 4 1/4 to 5 cups all-purpose flour

Frying:

- 1 quart (4 cups) vegetable oil for frying

Topping:

- 1 cup granulated sugar
- 2 teaspoons ground cinnamon
- Other toppings as desired (e.g., Nutella, chocolate sauce, lemon juice, maple syrup, fresh fruit, etc.)

Instructions

1. Prepare the Dough:
    - In a large bowl, combine the warm water, yeast, and a pinch of sugar. Let it stand for about 5 minutes, until frothy.
    - Add the warm milk, 1/3 cup of sugar, salt, vanilla extract, eggs, and vegetable oil to the yeast mixture. Stir to combine.
    - Gradually add the flour, one cup at a time, until the dough comes together and is no longer sticky. Knead the dough on a floured surface for about 6-8 minutes, until smooth and elastic.
    - Place the dough in a lightly oiled bowl, cover with a clean kitchen towel, and let it rise in a warm place until doubled in size, about 1 to 1 1/2 hours.
2. Shape the Dough:

- Punch down the dough to release the air. Divide it into 12 equal portions.
    - On a lightly floured surface, roll each portion into an oval shape about 1/4 inch thick. Stretch them slightly to resemble a beaver's tail.
3. Fry the BeaverTails:
    - In a deep fryer or large, deep skillet, heat the vegetable oil to 350°F (175°C).
    - Carefully place the shaped dough into the hot oil, one or two at a time, and fry until golden brown on both sides, about 1-2 minutes per side. Use a slotted spoon to remove them from the oil and drain on paper towels.
4. Add the Toppings:
    - While still warm, dip each BeaverTail in the cinnamon sugar mixture, ensuring an even coating.
    - Alternatively, you can add other toppings as desired, such as spreading with Nutella, drizzling with chocolate sauce, or adding a squeeze of lemon juice and a sprinkle of sugar.
5. Serve:
    - Serve the BeaverTails warm and enjoy this delicious treat!

These homemade BeaverTails are perfect for enjoying with family and friends and can be customized with a variety of toppings to suit your taste.

Maple Syrup Pie

Ingredients

Pie Crust:

- 1 1/4 cups all-purpose flour
- 1/4 teaspoon salt
- 1/2 cup unsalted butter, cold and cubed
- 2-3 tablespoons ice water

Filling:

- 1 cup pure maple syrup
- 1 cup heavy cream
- 1/2 cup brown sugar, packed
- 3 large eggs
- 3 tablespoons cornstarch
- 1 teaspoon vanilla extract
- 1/4 teaspoon salt

Instructions

1. Prepare the Pie Crust:
    - In a large bowl, whisk together the flour and salt.
    - Add the cold, cubed butter. Use a pastry cutter or your fingers to cut the butter into the flour until the mixture resembles coarse crumbs.
    - Gradually add the ice water, one tablespoon at a time, mixing with a fork until the dough begins to come together. Add just enough water for the dough to hold together without being sticky.
    - Form the dough into a disk, wrap in plastic wrap, and refrigerate for at least 30 minutes.
2. Roll Out the Dough:
    - On a lightly floured surface, roll out the chilled dough to fit a 9-inch pie plate, leaving some overhang.
    - Fit the dough into the pie plate, trim the excess, and crimp the edges. Refrigerate the crust while preparing the filling.
3. Preheat the Oven:
    - Preheat the oven to 350°F (175°C).
4. Prepare the Filling:

- In a medium saucepan, combine the maple syrup, heavy cream, and brown sugar. Heat over medium heat until the mixture comes to a gentle boil, stirring occasionally.
- In a separate bowl, whisk together the eggs, cornstarch, vanilla extract, and salt.
- Gradually pour the hot maple syrup mixture into the egg mixture, whisking constantly to prevent the eggs from curdling.
- Return the mixture to the saucepan and cook over medium heat, stirring constantly, until it thickens enough to coat the back of a spoon, about 5-7 minutes. Do not let it boil.

5. Assemble the Pie:
   - Pour the filling into the prepared pie crust.
6. Bake:
   - Bake in the preheated oven for 45-55 minutes, or until the filling is set and the crust is golden brown. The center should be slightly jiggly but will set as it cools.
   - If the crust edges brown too quickly, cover them with aluminum foil.
7. Cool:
   - Let the pie cool completely on a wire rack before serving. This allows the filling to fully set.

Serving Suggestion

- Serve the Maple Syrup Pie at room temperature or chilled, with a dollop of whipped cream or a scoop of vanilla ice cream if desired.

Enjoy your delicious homemade Maple Syrup Pie! This rich, sweet dessert is perfect for showcasing the unique flavor of pure maple syrup.

Blueberry Grunt

Ingredients

Blueberry Base:

- 4 cups fresh or frozen blueberries
- 1/2 cup granulated sugar
- 1/2 cup water
- 1 tablespoon lemon juice
- 1 teaspoon lemon zest
- 1 teaspoon ground cinnamon
- 1/4 teaspoon ground nutmeg

Dumplings:

- 2 cups all-purpose flour
- 2 tablespoons granulated sugar
- 1 tablespoon baking powder
- 1/2 teaspoon salt
- 1/4 cup unsalted butter, cold and cubed
- 3/4 cup milk (plus more if needed)
- 1 teaspoon vanilla extract

Instructions

1. Prepare the Blueberry Base:
    - In a large, deep skillet or saucepan, combine the blueberries, sugar, water, lemon juice, lemon zest, cinnamon, and nutmeg.
    - Bring the mixture to a simmer over medium heat, stirring occasionally until the sugar dissolves and the berries release their juices, about 5-10 minutes.
2. Prepare the Dumpling Dough:
    - In a large bowl, whisk together the flour, sugar, baking powder, and salt.
    - Add the cold, cubed butter. Use a pastry cutter or your fingers to cut the butter into the flour until the mixture resembles coarse crumbs.
    - Stir in the milk and vanilla extract until just combined. The dough should be slightly sticky; if it's too dry, add a little more milk, a tablespoon at a time.
3. Cook the Dumplings:

- Drop spoonfuls of the dumpling dough over the simmering blueberry mixture. The dumplings should be roughly 2 inches in diameter and spaced apart as they will expand while cooking.
- Cover the skillet with a tight-fitting lid and reduce the heat to low. Let the mixture simmer, covered, for about 15-20 minutes, or until the dumplings are puffed up and cooked through. Avoid lifting the lid during this time to ensure the dumplings steam properly.

4. Serve:
    - Spoon the blueberry mixture and dumplings into bowls and serve warm.

Serving Suggestions

- Blueberry Grunt is delicious on its own, but you can also serve it with a scoop of vanilla ice cream or a dollop of whipped cream for extra indulgence.

Enjoy your homemade Blueberry Grunt! This comforting dessert showcases the natural sweetness of blueberries and is perfect for any occasion.

Flapper Pie

Ingredients

Graham Cracker Crust:

- 1 1/2 cups graham cracker crumbs
- 1/4 cup granulated sugar
- 1/2 cup unsalted butter, melted

Custard Filling:

- 1/2 cup granulated sugar
- 1/4 cup cornstarch
- 1/4 teaspoon salt
- 3 cups whole milk
- 4 large egg yolks
- 1 teaspoon vanilla extract

Meringue Topping:

- 4 large egg whites, at room temperature
- 1/4 teaspoon cream of tartar
- 1/2 cup granulated sugar
- 1/2 teaspoon vanilla extract

Instructions

1. Prepare the Graham Cracker Crust:
    - Preheat the oven to 350°F (175°C).
    - In a bowl, combine the graham cracker crumbs, sugar, and melted butter until well mixed.
    - Press the mixture firmly into the bottom and up the sides of a 9-inch pie dish.
    - Bake the crust in the preheated oven for 8-10 minutes, or until lightly golden. Remove from the oven and let it cool completely.
2. Prepare the Custard Filling:
    - In a medium saucepan, whisk together the sugar, cornstarch, and salt.
    - Gradually whisk in the milk until smooth. Place the saucepan over medium heat.

- Cook the mixture, stirring constantly, until it thickens and comes to a gentle boil, about 5-7 minutes.
- In a separate bowl, lightly beat the egg yolks. Gradually whisk in about 1/2 cup of the hot milk mixture to temper the eggs.
- Pour the tempered egg mixture back into the saucepan with the remaining milk mixture, whisking constantly.
- Cook for an additional 2-3 minutes, stirring constantly, until the custard is thickened.
- Remove from heat and stir in the vanilla extract.
- Pour the custard filling into the cooled graham cracker crust, spreading it evenly.
3. Prepare the Meringue Topping:
    - In a clean, dry bowl, beat the egg whites and cream of tartar with an electric mixer on medium speed until soft peaks form.
    - Gradually add the sugar, about a tablespoon at a time, while continuing to beat on high speed. Beat until stiff, glossy peaks form.
    - Beat in the vanilla extract.
4. Assemble and Bake:
    - Spoon the meringue over the custard filling, spreading it to the edges of the pie to seal in the custard completely.
    - Use the back of a spoon to create peaks in the meringue.
    - Bake the pie in the preheated oven for 10-12 minutes, or until the meringue is golden brown.
5. Cool and Serve:
    - Let the pie cool completely on a wire rack before slicing and serving.

Serving Suggestions

- Serve the Flapper Pie chilled or at room temperature for best flavor and texture.

Enjoy your homemade Flapper Pie! It's a delightful dessert that combines creamy custard, crunchy crust, and fluffy meringue—a true Canadian classic.

Maple Fudge

Ingredients:

- 1 cup pure maple syrup
- 1 cup granulated sugar
- 1 cup heavy cream
- 2 tablespoons unsalted butter, plus extra for greasing the pan
- 1 teaspoon vanilla extract
- Optional: Chopped nuts for topping (such as pecans or walnuts)

Instructions:

1. Prepare the Pan:
   - Grease an 8x8-inch square baking pan with butter or line it with parchment paper, leaving an overhang on the sides for easy removal of the fudge later.
2. Cook the Fudge:
   - In a medium saucepan, combine the maple syrup, granulated sugar, and heavy cream over medium heat. Stir constantly until the sugar is dissolved and the mixture comes to a boil.
   - Attach a candy thermometer to the side of the saucepan. Let the mixture cook, without stirring, until it reaches the soft ball stage, which is around 235°F to 240°F (113°C to 116°C). This usually takes about 15-20 minutes.
   - Once the desired temperature is reached, remove the saucepan from the heat.
3. Cool and Beat:
   - Add the butter and vanilla extract to the saucepan. Do not stir.
   - Let the mixture cool in the saucepan without stirring until it reaches about 110°F (43°C) or until the bottom of the saucepan is just warm to the touch.
   - Once cooled, beat the mixture vigorously with a wooden spoon or a handheld mixer until it thickens and starts to lose its gloss. This usually takes about 5-10 minutes.
   - If desired, fold in chopped nuts at this stage for added texture.
4. Set the Fudge:
   - Pour the beaten fudge mixture into the prepared baking pan, spreading it evenly with a spatula.
   - Let the fudge cool and set at room temperature for at least 2-3 hours, or until firm.

5. Slice and Serve:
    - Once the fudge is completely set, use a sharp knife to slice it into squares.
    - Serve and enjoy!

Storage:

- Store the maple fudge in an airtight container at room temperature for up to a week. You can also refrigerate it for longer storage, but let it come to room temperature before serving for the best texture.

Maple fudge makes a wonderful homemade treat or a delightful gift for friends and family, especially during the holiday season or maple syrup season in Canada!

Date Squares

Ingredients:

Date Filling:

- 2 cups pitted dates, chopped
- 1 cup water
- 1 tablespoon lemon juice
- 1/4 cup granulated sugar

Oatmeal Crumble Layers:

- 1 1/2 cups old-fashioned rolled oats
- 1 1/2 cups all-purpose flour
- 1 cup packed brown sugar
- 1/2 teaspoon baking soda
- 1/2 teaspoon salt
- 3/4 cup unsalted butter, cold and cubed

Instructions:

1. Prepare the Date Filling:
    - In a medium saucepan, combine the chopped dates, water, lemon juice, and granulated sugar.
    - Cook the mixture over medium heat, stirring occasionally, until the dates are softened and the mixture has thickened to a jam-like consistency, about 10-15 minutes.
    - Remove from heat and let the date filling cool slightly.
2. Prepare the Oatmeal Crumble Layers:
    - Preheat the oven to 350°F (175°C). Grease or line a 9x9-inch square baking pan with parchment paper, leaving an overhang on the sides for easy removal.
    - In a large mixing bowl, combine the rolled oats, all-purpose flour, brown sugar, baking soda, and salt.
    - Add the cold, cubed butter to the dry ingredients. Use a pastry cutter or your fingers to cut the butter into the mixture until it resembles coarse crumbs and the butter is well distributed.
3. Assemble the Date Squares:

- Press half of the oatmeal crumble mixture firmly and evenly into the bottom of the prepared baking pan.
- Spread the cooled date filling over the oatmeal layer, spreading it out evenly.
- Sprinkle the remaining oatmeal crumble mixture over the date filling, covering it completely.

4. **Bake:**
    - Bake the date squares in the preheated oven for 30-35 minutes, or until the top is golden brown and the edges are slightly bubbly.
    - Remove from the oven and let the date squares cool completely in the pan on a wire rack.

5. **Slice and Serve:**
    - Once cooled, use the parchment paper overhang to lift the date squares out of the pan.
    - Cut into squares or bars using a sharp knife.
    - Serve and enjoy!

Storage:

- Date squares can be stored in an airtight container at room temperature for up to 5 days. They can also be frozen for longer storage, wrapped tightly in plastic wrap and aluminum foil.

These date squares are perfect for serving as a sweet treat with a cup of coffee or tea, or for bringing to potlucks and gatherings to share with friends and family.

Pouding Chômeur

Ingredients:

For the Cake Batter:

- 1 cup all-purpose flour
- 1 teaspoon baking powder
- 1/4 teaspoon salt
- 1/4 cup unsalted butter, softened
- 1/2 cup granulated sugar
- 1 large egg
- 1/2 cup milk

For the Sauce:

- 1 cup maple syrup
- 1 cup brown sugar
- 1 cup water
- 1/4 cup unsalted butter

Instructions:

1. Preheat the Oven:
   - Preheat your oven to 350°F (175°C). Grease a 9-inch square baking dish or a similar-sized ovenproof dish.
2. Prepare the Cake Batter:
   - In a medium bowl, whisk together the flour, baking powder, and salt.
   - In a separate large mixing bowl, cream together the softened butter and granulated sugar until light and fluffy.
   - Beat in the egg until well combined.
   - Gradually add the flour mixture to the creamed mixture, alternating with the milk, until you have a smooth batter.
3. Make the Sauce:
   - In a saucepan, combine the maple syrup, brown sugar, water, and butter.
   - Bring the mixture to a boil over medium heat, stirring constantly.
   - Reduce the heat and let it simmer for 5 minutes, stirring occasionally.
4. Assemble the Pudding:
   - Pour the hot sauce into the prepared baking dish.

- Spoon the cake batter over the sauce in the baking dish, spreading it out as evenly as possible.
5. Bake:
    - Place the baking dish in the preheated oven and bake for 30-35 minutes, or until the cake is golden brown and a toothpick inserted into the center comes out clean.
6. Serve:
    - Let the Pouding Chômeur cool slightly before serving.
    - Serve warm, spooning some of the sauce over each serving.

Serving Suggestions:

- Pouding Chômeur is often served warm with a dollop of whipped cream or a scoop of vanilla ice cream for extra indulgence.
- You can also garnish it with chopped nuts or a sprinkle of powdered sugar before serving.

This comforting and simple dessert is perfect for cozy evenings or special occasions, and it's sure to be a hit with anyone who tries it!

Apple Crisp

Ingredients:

For the Apple Filling:

- 6 cups apples (such as Granny Smith, Honeycrisp, or a mix), peeled, cored, and sliced
- 1/4 cup granulated sugar
- 1 tablespoon lemon juice
- 1 teaspoon ground cinnamon
- 1/4 teaspoon ground nutmeg
- 1/4 teaspoon ground cloves (optional)

For the Crumble Topping:

- 1 cup old-fashioned rolled oats
- 1/2 cup all-purpose flour
- 1/2 cup packed brown sugar
- 1/2 teaspoon ground cinnamon
- 1/4 teaspoon salt
- 1/2 cup unsalted butter, melted

Instructions:

1. Preheat the Oven:
    - Preheat your oven to 350°F (175°C). Grease a 9x9-inch baking dish or a similar-sized ovenproof dish.
2. Prepare the Apple Filling:
    - In a large bowl, combine the sliced apples, granulated sugar, lemon juice, cinnamon, nutmeg, and cloves (if using). Toss until the apples are evenly coated with the sugar and spices.
3. Make the Crumble Topping:
    - In another bowl, combine the rolled oats, flour, brown sugar, cinnamon, and salt.
    - Pour the melted butter over the oat mixture and stir until it is evenly moistened and forms clumps.
4. Assemble and Bake:
    - Spread the apple mixture evenly in the prepared baking dish.
    - Sprinkle the crumble topping over the apples, covering them completely.

5. Bake:
    - Place the baking dish in the preheated oven and bake for 40-45 minutes, or until the apples are tender and the topping is golden brown and crisp.
6. Serve:
    - Let the apple crisp cool for a few minutes before serving.
    - Serve warm, optionally topped with a scoop of vanilla ice cream or a dollop of whipped cream.

Serving Suggestions:

- Apple crisp is delicious on its own, but you can also serve it with a drizzle of caramel sauce for extra sweetness.
- Feel free to customize the recipe by adding chopped nuts (such as pecans or walnuts) to the crumble topping for added crunch and flavor.

This warm and comforting dessert is perfect for any occasion, especially during the fall season when apples are in abundance. Enjoy!

Maple Butter Tart Squares

Ingredients:

For the Shortbread Crust:

- 1 cup all-purpose flour
- 1/4 cup granulated sugar
- 1/2 cup unsalted butter, cold and cubed

For the Filling:

- 2/3 cup pure maple syrup
- 1/2 cup packed brown sugar
- 1/4 cup unsalted butter, melted
- 2 large eggs, beaten
- 1 teaspoon vanilla extract
- 1 tablespoon all-purpose flour
- 1/4 teaspoon salt
- 1/2 cup chopped pecans or walnuts (optional)

Instructions:

1. Preheat the Oven:
    - Preheat your oven to 350°F (175°C). Grease or line an 8x8-inch baking pan with parchment paper, leaving an overhang on the sides for easy removal.
2. Prepare the Shortbread Crust:
    - In a mixing bowl, combine the flour and granulated sugar. Cut in the cold, cubed butter using a pastry cutter or your fingers until the mixture resembles coarse crumbs.
    - Press the mixture evenly into the bottom of the prepared baking pan.
3. Bake the Crust:
    - Bake the crust in the preheated oven for 15-20 minutes, or until lightly golden brown. Remove from the oven and set aside.
4. Prepare the Filling:
    - In a medium bowl, whisk together the maple syrup, brown sugar, melted butter, beaten eggs, and vanilla extract until well combined.
    - Stir in the flour and salt until smooth. If using, fold in the chopped nuts.
5. Assemble and Bake:
    - Pour the filling over the baked shortbread crust, spreading it out evenly.

- - Return the pan to the oven and bake for an additional 20-25 minutes, or until the filling is set and the edges are lightly golden brown.
6. **Cool and Serve:**
   - Allow the Maple Butter Tart Squares to cool completely in the pan on a wire rack.
   - Once cooled, use the parchment paper overhang to lift the squares out of the pan.
   - Cut into squares or bars using a sharp knife.
   - Serve and enjoy!

Serving Suggestions:

- These Maple Butter Tart Squares are delicious on their own, but you can also serve them with a scoop of vanilla ice cream or a dollop of whipped cream for extra indulgence.
- Dust with powdered sugar before serving for a decorative touch.

These squares are perfect for sharing at gatherings, potlucks, or as a special treat for maple syrup lovers. Enjoy the rich, gooey goodness!

Snow Taffy

Ingredients:

- Pure maple syrup (preferably dark or amber grade)

Instructions:

1. Prepare the Snow:
    - Choose a clean, fresh layer of snow. Make sure it's free from any debris or dirt. Pack the snow down lightly to create a smooth surface for pouring the hot syrup.
2. Heat the Maple Syrup:
    - In a small saucepan, heat the maple syrup over medium heat until it reaches the soft ball stage, which is around 235°F to 240°F (113°C to 116°C) on a candy thermometer. This usually takes about 7-10 minutes.
    - It's important to keep an eye on the syrup and stir it occasionally to prevent it from boiling over.
3. Pour the Syrup:
    - Once the syrup reaches the soft ball stage, remove it from the heat. Carefully pour small lines or puddles of hot syrup onto the packed snow. Leave some space between each pour to prevent them from merging together.
4. Let it Cool:
    - Allow the hot syrup to cool and solidify on the snow for a few seconds to a minute. You'll notice that it starts to firm up and become taffy-like in texture.
5. Roll and Enjoy:
    - Use a popsicle stick or a fork to gently lift the edges of the cooled syrup from the snow.
    - Quickly roll the taffy around the stick or fork to create a lollipop-like shape.
    - Enjoy your homemade snow taffy immediately before it melts or hardens too much.

Tips:

- Work quickly once you pour the syrup onto the snow, as it will start to solidify rapidly.
- Be careful when handling the hot syrup to avoid burns.

- You can experiment with different shapes and sizes of snow taffy by pouring the syrup in various patterns or using different utensils for rolling.

Snow taffy is a fun and delicious winter treat that's perfect for enjoying with family and friends, especially on a snowy day!

Caramelized Maple Apple Tart

Ingredients:

For the Pastry Crust:

- 1 1/4 cups all-purpose flour
- 1/2 cup unsalted butter, cold and cubed
- 1/4 cup granulated sugar
- 1/4 teaspoon salt
- 2-4 tablespoons ice water

For the Apple Filling:

- 4-5 medium apples, peeled, cored, and thinly sliced (such as Granny Smith or Honeycrisp)
- 1/4 cup unsalted butter
- 1/2 cup maple syrup
- 1/4 cup brown sugar
- 1 teaspoon ground cinnamon
- 1/4 teaspoon ground nutmeg
- 1/4 teaspoon salt

Instructions:

1. Prepare the Pastry Crust:
    - In a food processor, combine the flour, sugar, and salt. Pulse to mix.
    - Add the cold, cubed butter to the flour mixture. Pulse until the mixture resembles coarse crumbs.
    - Gradually add the ice water, one tablespoon at a time, and pulse until the dough comes together and forms a ball.
    - Shape the dough into a disk, wrap it in plastic wrap, and refrigerate for at least 30 minutes.
2. Preheat the Oven:
    - Preheat your oven to 375°F (190°C).
3. Prepare the Apple Filling:
    - In a large skillet, melt the butter over medium heat.
    - Add the sliced apples to the skillet and cook for 5-7 minutes, or until slightly softened.

- Stir in the maple syrup, brown sugar, cinnamon, nutmeg, and salt. Cook for an additional 5 minutes, stirring occasionally, until the apples are caramelized and tender. Remove from heat and let cool slightly.
4. Roll Out the Dough:
    - On a lightly floured surface, roll out the chilled pastry dough into a circle large enough to fit into a 9-inch tart pan. Press the dough into the bottom and sides of the tart pan, trimming any excess.
5. Assemble and Bake:
    - Arrange the caramelized apple slices in an even layer over the pastry crust.
    - Pour any remaining maple caramel sauce from the skillet over the apples.
    - Bake in the preheated oven for 30-35 minutes, or until the crust is golden brown and the apples are bubbling and caramelized.
6. Cool and Serve:
    - Let the tart cool slightly before slicing and serving.
    - Serve warm or at room temperature, optionally with a scoop of vanilla ice cream or a dollop of whipped cream.

Optional Garnish:

- Drizzle additional maple syrup over the top of the tart before serving for extra sweetness and flavor.

This Caramelized Maple Apple Tart is a delicious and elegant dessert that's perfect for any occasion, especially during the fall season when apples are in abundance. Enjoy the rich caramelized flavors and the comforting aroma of cinnamon and maple syrup!

Maple Walnut Ice Cream

Ingredients:

- 2 cups heavy cream
- 1 cup whole milk
- 3/4 cup pure maple syrup
- 4 large egg yolks
- 1/2 teaspoon vanilla extract
- Pinch of salt
- 1/2 cup chopped walnuts, toasted

Instructions:

1. Prepare the Ice Cream Base:
    - In a saucepan, heat the heavy cream, whole milk, and maple syrup over medium heat until it just begins to simmer. Do not let it boil.
    - In a separate bowl, whisk the egg yolks until smooth.
    - Gradually pour about half of the hot cream mixture into the egg yolks, whisking constantly to temper the yolks.
    - Pour the tempered egg mixture back into the saucepan with the remaining cream mixture, whisking constantly.
2. Cook the Custard:
    - Cook the mixture over medium heat, stirring constantly with a wooden spoon or heatproof spatula, until it thickens slightly and coats the back of the spoon. This usually takes about 5-7 minutes. Do not let it boil.
3. Strain the Custard:
    - Remove the saucepan from heat and strain the custard through a fine-mesh sieve into a clean bowl to remove any cooked egg bits.
    - Stir in the vanilla extract and a pinch of salt. Let the custard cool to room temperature, then cover and refrigerate until completely chilled, preferably overnight.
4. Churn the Ice Cream:
    - Once the custard is thoroughly chilled, churn it in an ice cream maker according to the manufacturer's instructions until it reaches a soft-serve consistency.
    - During the last few minutes of churning, add the chopped toasted walnuts and continue churning until evenly distributed.
5. Freeze the Ice Cream:

- Transfer the churned ice cream to a freezer-safe container. Press a piece of parchment paper directly onto the surface of the ice cream to prevent ice crystals from forming.
- Freeze the ice cream for at least 4 hours or until firm.
6. Serve and Enjoy:
    - Once the ice cream is fully frozen, scoop it into bowls or cones and serve immediately.
    - Garnish with additional toasted walnuts or a drizzle of maple syrup if desired.

Tips:

- To toast walnuts, spread them in a single layer on a baking sheet and bake in a preheated 350°F (175°C) oven for 8-10 minutes, or until fragrant and lightly golden brown. Let them cool before chopping and adding to the ice cream.
- For a stronger maple flavor, you can use a combination of maple syrup and maple extract.

This homemade maple walnut ice cream is a decadent treat that's perfect for enjoying on its own or as a delicious topping for pies, cakes, or waffles. Enjoy the creamy texture and delightful combination of flavors!

Persimmon Pudding

Ingredients:

- 2 cups ripe persimmon pulp (from about 4-5 ripe persimmons)
- 1 cup granulated sugar
- 2 large eggs
- 1 cup all-purpose flour
- 1 teaspoon baking soda
- 1/4 teaspoon salt
- 1 teaspoon ground cinnamon
- 1/2 teaspoon ground nutmeg
- 1/2 teaspoon ground ginger
- 1/2 cup chopped walnuts or pecans (optional)
- Whipped cream or vanilla ice cream, for serving (optional)

Instructions:

1. Prepare the Persimmon Pulp:
    - Start by preparing the persimmons. Scoop out the pulp from ripe persimmons and discard any seeds or tough parts. Mash the pulp with a fork or blend it in a food processor until smooth. You should have about 2 cups of persimmon pulp.
2. Preheat the Oven:
    - Preheat your oven to 350°F (175°C). Grease a 9x9-inch baking dish or a similar-sized ovenproof dish.
3. Mix the Wet Ingredients:
    - In a large mixing bowl, combine the persimmon pulp, granulated sugar, and eggs. Mix until well combined.
4. Add the Dry Ingredients:
    - In a separate bowl, whisk together the flour, baking soda, salt, cinnamon, nutmeg, and ginger.
    - Gradually add the dry ingredients to the wet ingredients, stirring until just combined. Be careful not to overmix.
    - If using, fold in the chopped nuts until evenly distributed throughout the batter.
5. Bake the Pudding:
    - Pour the batter into the prepared baking dish, spreading it out evenly.

- Bake in the preheated oven for 40-45 minutes, or until the pudding is set and a toothpick inserted into the center comes out clean.
6. Cool and Serve:
    - Let the persimmon pudding cool slightly in the baking dish before serving.
    - Serve warm, optionally topped with whipped cream or vanilla ice cream, for extra indulgence.

Serving Suggestions:

- Persimmon pudding is delicious on its own, but you can also serve it with a dusting of powdered sugar or a drizzle of caramel sauce for added sweetness.
- Enjoy a slice of persimmon pudding with a cup of hot tea or coffee for a cozy and comforting dessert experience.

This moist and flavorful persimmon pudding is sure to be a hit with family and friends, showcasing the unique taste of ripe persimmons in a delightful dessert.

Rhubarb Crisp

Ingredients:

For the Rhubarb Filling:

- 4 cups chopped rhubarb (about 1-inch pieces)
- 1/2 cup granulated sugar
- 2 tablespoons all-purpose flour
- 1 teaspoon vanilla extract
- Zest of 1 orange (optional)

For the Crisp Topping:

- 1 cup old-fashioned rolled oats
- 1/2 cup all-purpose flour
- 1/2 cup packed brown sugar
- 1/2 teaspoon ground cinnamon
- 1/4 teaspoon salt
- 1/2 cup unsalted butter, melted

Instructions:

1. Preheat the Oven:
    - Preheat your oven to 350°F (175°C). Grease a 9x9-inch baking dish or a similar-sized ovenproof dish.
2. Prepare the Rhubarb Filling:
    - In a large mixing bowl, combine the chopped rhubarb, granulated sugar, flour, vanilla extract, and orange zest (if using). Toss until the rhubarb is evenly coated with the sugar mixture.
3. Make the Crisp Topping:
    - In another bowl, combine the rolled oats, flour, brown sugar, cinnamon, and salt.
    - Pour the melted butter over the oat mixture and stir until well combined and crumbly.
4. Assemble the Crisp:
    - Spread the rhubarb filling evenly in the prepared baking dish.
    - Sprinkle the crisp topping over the rhubarb filling, covering it completely.
5. Bake:

- - Place the baking dish in the preheated oven and bake for 35-40 minutes, or until the rhubarb is tender and the crisp topping is golden brown and crisp.
6. **Cool and Serve:**
    - Let the rhubarb crisp cool for a few minutes before serving.
    - Serve warm, optionally with a scoop of vanilla ice cream or a dollop of whipped cream.

Serving Suggestions:

- Rhubarb crisp is delicious on its own, but you can also serve it with a drizzle of caramel sauce or a sprinkle of powdered sugar for extra sweetness.
- Enjoy a slice of rhubarb crisp with a cup of tea or coffee for a delightful afternoon treat.

This rhubarb crisp is a wonderful dessert to make during the spring and summer months when rhubarb is in season. The combination of tart rhubarb and sweet, crunchy topping is sure to be a hit with everyone!

Blueberry Buckle

Ingredients:

For the Streusel Topping:

- 1/2 cup all-purpose flour
- 1/4 cup granulated sugar
- 1/4 cup packed brown sugar
- 1/2 teaspoon ground cinnamon
- 1/4 cup unsalted butter, cold and cubed

For the Cake Batter:

- 2 cups all-purpose flour
- 2 teaspoons baking powder
- 1/2 teaspoon salt
- 1/2 cup unsalted butter, softened
- 3/4 cup granulated sugar
- 2 large eggs
- 1 teaspoon vanilla extract
- 1/2 cup milk
- 2 cups fresh or frozen blueberries (if using frozen, do not thaw)

Instructions:

1. Preheat the Oven:
    - Preheat your oven to 375°F (190°C). Grease a 9x9-inch baking dish or a similar-sized ovenproof dish.
2. Prepare the Streusel Topping:
    - In a small bowl, combine the flour, granulated sugar, brown sugar, and cinnamon for the streusel topping.
    - Add the cold, cubed butter to the mixture. Use a pastry cutter or your fingers to cut the butter into the dry ingredients until the mixture resembles coarse crumbs. Set aside.
3. Prepare the Cake Batter:
    - In a medium bowl, whisk together the flour, baking powder, and salt for the cake batter.
    - In a separate large mixing bowl, cream together the softened butter and granulated sugar until light and fluffy.

- Beat in the eggs, one at a time, until well combined. Stir in the vanilla extract.
- Gradually add the dry ingredients to the creamed mixture, alternating with the milk, until just combined. Do not overmix.
- Gently fold in the blueberries until evenly distributed throughout the batter.
4. Assemble and Bake:
    - Spread the cake batter evenly into the prepared baking dish.
    - Sprinkle the streusel topping evenly over the top of the batter.
5. Bake:
    - Place the baking dish in the preheated oven and bake for 35-40 minutes, or until the cake is golden brown and a toothpick inserted into the center comes out clean.
6. Cool and Serve:
    - Let the blueberry buckle cool slightly in the baking dish before serving.
    - Serve warm or at room temperature, optionally with a scoop of vanilla ice cream or a dollop of whipped cream.

Serving Suggestions:

- Blueberry buckle is delicious on its own, but you can also serve it with a dusting of powdered sugar or a drizzle of maple syrup for extra sweetness.
- Enjoy a slice of blueberry buckle with a cup of tea or coffee for a delightful afternoon treat.

This blueberry buckle is a perfect dessert to make during the summer when blueberries are in season, but it's equally enjoyable any time of the year. The combination of tender cake, juicy blueberries, and crumbly streusel topping is sure to be a hit with everyone!

Maple Shortbread Cookies

Ingredients:

- 1 cup unsalted butter, softened
- 1/2 cup granulated sugar
- 1/4 cup pure maple syrup
- 2 cups all-purpose flour
- 1/4 teaspoon salt
- Optional: Additional granulated sugar for sprinkling on top

Instructions:

1. Preheat the Oven:
    - Preheat your oven to 325°F (160°C). Line a baking sheet with parchment paper or silicone baking mat.
2. Cream the Butter and Sugar:
    - In a large mixing bowl, cream together the softened butter and granulated sugar until light and fluffy.
3. Add Maple Syrup:
    - Mix in the pure maple syrup until well combined.
4. Mix in Flour and Salt:
    - Gradually add the flour and salt to the butter mixture, mixing until a dough forms. Be careful not to overmix.
5. Shape the Dough:
    - Transfer the dough onto a lightly floured surface. Shape the dough into a disk and wrap it in plastic wrap. Chill in the refrigerator for about 30 minutes to firm up.
6. Roll and Cut the Cookies:
    - Once chilled, roll out the dough on a floured surface to about 1/4 inch thickness. Use cookie cutters to cut out shapes.
    - Place the cut-out cookies onto the prepared baking sheet, leaving some space between each cookie.
7. Bake:
    - Bake the cookies in the preheated oven for 12-15 minutes, or until the edges are lightly golden brown.
8. Optional: Sprinkle with Sugar:
    - If desired, while the cookies are still warm, sprinkle them with additional granulated sugar for a sparkly finish.

9. Cool and Serve:
    - Let the cookies cool on the baking sheet for a few minutes before transferring them to a wire rack to cool completely.
    - Once cooled, serve and enjoy!

Tips:

- For an extra maple flavor, you can brush the tops of the cookies with a little maple syrup before baking.
- These cookies can be stored in an airtight container at room temperature for several days. They also freeze well for longer storage.

These maple shortbread cookies are perfect for enjoying with a cup of tea or coffee, or for gifting to friends and family during the holidays or any time of year!

Pumpkin Pie

Ingredients:

For the Pie Crust:

- 1 1/4 cups all-purpose flour
- 1/2 teaspoon salt
- 1/2 teaspoon granulated sugar
- 1/2 cup unsalted butter, cold and cubed
- 3-4 tablespoons ice water

For the Pumpkin Filling:

- 1 (15-ounce) can pumpkin puree (about 1 3/4 cups)
- 3/4 cup granulated sugar
- 2 large eggs
- 1 teaspoon ground cinnamon
- 1/2 teaspoon ground ginger
- 1/4 teaspoon ground cloves
- 1/2 teaspoon ground nutmeg
- 1/2 teaspoon salt
- 1 cup evaporated milk or half-and-half

Instructions:

1. Prepare the Pie Crust:
    - In a food processor, combine the flour, salt, and sugar. Pulse to mix.
    - Add the cold, cubed butter to the flour mixture. Pulse until the mixture resembles coarse crumbs.
    - Gradually add the ice water, one tablespoon at a time, and pulse until the dough comes together and forms a ball.
    - Shape the dough into a disk, wrap it in plastic wrap, and refrigerate for at least 30 minutes.
2. Preheat the Oven:
    - Preheat your oven to 425°F (220°C). Place a baking sheet in the oven to preheat as well.
3. Roll Out the Dough:

- On a lightly floured surface, roll out the chilled dough into a circle large enough to fit into a 9-inch pie dish. Transfer the dough to the pie dish and trim any excess. Crimp the edges as desired.
4. Prepare the Pumpkin Filling:
    - In a large mixing bowl, whisk together the pumpkin puree, granulated sugar, eggs, spices (cinnamon, ginger, cloves, nutmeg), and salt until well combined.
    - Gradually stir in the evaporated milk or half-and-half until smooth.
5. Assemble and Bake:
    - Pour the pumpkin filling into the prepared pie crust.
    - Carefully place the pie on the preheated baking sheet in the oven.
    - Bake at 425°F (220°C) for 15 minutes, then reduce the oven temperature to 350°F (175°C) and continue baking for 40-50 minutes, or until the filling is set and a knife inserted near the center comes out clean.
6. Cool and Serve:
    - Let the pumpkin pie cool completely on a wire rack before serving.
    - Serve slices of pumpkin pie with whipped cream or vanilla ice cream, if desired.

Tips:

- To prevent the edges of the pie crust from over-browning, you can cover them with aluminum foil or a pie crust shield during baking.
- For added flavor and texture, you can sprinkle chopped pecans or walnuts over the top of the pie before baking.

This classic pumpkin pie is sure to be a hit at any holiday gathering or family dinner. Enjoy the warm spices and creamy texture of this comforting dessert!

Maple Cake

Ingredients:

For the Cake:

- 2 cups all-purpose flour
- 2 teaspoons baking powder
- 1/2 teaspoon baking soda
- 1/4 teaspoon salt
- 1/2 cup unsalted butter, softened
- 1 cup granulated sugar
- 2 large eggs
- 1 teaspoon vanilla extract
- 3/4 cup pure maple syrup
- 1/2 cup buttermilk

For the Maple Glaze:

- 1/4 cup unsalted butter
- 1/4 cup pure maple syrup
- 1 cup confectioners' sugar, sifted
- 1/2 teaspoon vanilla extract

Instructions:

1. Preheat the Oven:
    - Preheat your oven to 350°F (175°C). Grease and flour a 9-inch round cake pan or line it with parchment paper.
2. Prepare the Cake Batter:
    - In a medium bowl, whisk together the flour, baking powder, baking soda, and salt.
    - In a large mixing bowl, cream together the softened butter and granulated sugar until light and fluffy.
    - Beat in the eggs, one at a time, until well combined. Stir in the vanilla extract.
    - Gradually add the maple syrup to the butter mixture, mixing until smooth.
    - Alternately add the dry ingredients and buttermilk to the butter mixture, beginning and ending with the dry ingredients. Mix until just combined.
3. Bake the Cake:

- Pour the cake batter into the prepared cake pan and spread it out evenly.
- Bake in the preheated oven for 25-30 minutes, or until a toothpick inserted into the center of the cake comes out clean.
- Remove the cake from the oven and let it cool in the pan for 10 minutes before transferring it to a wire rack to cool completely.

4. Prepare the Maple Glaze:
   - In a small saucepan, melt the butter over medium heat. Stir in the maple syrup.
   - Remove the saucepan from the heat and whisk in the confectioners' sugar and vanilla extract until smooth.

5. Glaze the Cake:
   - Once the cake has cooled completely, place it on a serving plate or cake stand.
   - Drizzle the maple glaze over the top of the cake, allowing it to drip down the sides.

6. Serve and Enjoy:
   - Slice the maple cake and serve it on its own or with a dollop of whipped cream or a scoop of vanilla ice cream, if desired.

Tips:

- For added texture and flavor, you can sprinkle chopped pecans or walnuts over the top of the cake before adding the glaze.
- Make sure the cake is completely cooled before adding the glaze to prevent it from melting.

This maple cake is perfect for any occasion, from casual gatherings to special celebrations. Enjoy the rich, sweet flavor of maple in every bite!

Bannock

Ingredients:

- 2 cups all-purpose flour
- 2 teaspoons baking powder
- 1/2 teaspoon salt
- 1/4 cup vegetable oil or melted butter
- 1/2 cup water (or more, as needed)

Instructions:

1. Mix Dry Ingredients:
    - In a large mixing bowl, whisk together the all-purpose flour, baking powder, and salt until well combined.
2. Add Wet Ingredients:
    - Make a well in the center of the dry ingredients and pour in the vegetable oil or melted butter.
    - Gradually add the water, a little at a time, while stirring with a wooden spoon or your hands. Mix until a soft dough forms. Add more water if necessary to bring the dough together.
3. Knead the Dough:
    - Turn the dough out onto a lightly floured surface and knead it gently for a few minutes until smooth. Be careful not to overwork the dough.
4. Shape the Bannock:
    - Divide the dough into smaller portions and shape each portion into a round flat disk, about 1/2 inch thick. You can also shape the dough into individual small rounds or one large round, depending on your preference.
5. Cook the Bannock:
    - Heat a lightly greased skillet or griddle over medium heat.
    - Once the skillet is hot, carefully transfer the shaped bannock dough to the skillet.
    - Cook the bannock for 3-4 minutes on each side, or until golden brown and cooked through. You may need to adjust the heat as necessary to prevent burning.
6. Serve and Enjoy:
    - Once cooked, transfer the bannock to a plate and serve warm.
    - Bannock can be enjoyed on its own, served with butter or jam, or used as a base for savory toppings like chili or stew.

Variations:

- For a sweeter version of bannock, you can add a couple of tablespoons of sugar to the dry ingredients before mixing.
- You can also incorporate additional flavorings such as herbs, spices, or grated cheese into the dough for a more savory option.

Bannock is a versatile bread that can be enjoyed in various ways and adapted to suit different tastes and preferences. It's perfect for outdoor gatherings, camping trips, or as a comforting bread to enjoy at home.

Maple Cream Pie

Ingredients:

For the Pie Crust:

- 1 9-inch unbaked pie crust (store-bought or homemade)

For the Maple Cream Filling:

- 1 cup pure maple syrup
- 1 cup heavy cream
- 1/4 cup cornstarch
- 1/4 cup granulated sugar
- 1/4 teaspoon salt
- 4 large egg yolks
- 2 tablespoons unsalted butter
- 1 teaspoon vanilla extract

For Garnish (optional):

- Whipped cream
- Maple syrup

Instructions:

1. Preheat the Oven:
   - Preheat your oven to 375°F (190°C).
2. Prepare the Pie Crust:
   - Line a 9-inch pie plate with the unbaked pie crust. Crimp the edges as desired. Prick the bottom of the crust with a fork to prevent bubbling during baking.
   - Partially bake the pie crust in the preheated oven for about 10 minutes, or until it's just starting to set. Remove from the oven and set aside.
3. Prepare the Maple Cream Filling:
   - In a medium saucepan, whisk together the maple syrup, heavy cream, cornstarch, granulated sugar, and salt until smooth.
   - Place the saucepan over medium heat and cook the mixture, stirring constantly, until it thickens and comes to a gentle boil.
   - In a separate bowl, whisk the egg yolks until smooth. Gradually whisk in a small amount of the hot maple mixture to temper the yolks.

- Pour the tempered egg yolk mixture back into the saucepan with the remaining maple mixture, whisking constantly.
    - Continue cooking and stirring for an additional 2-3 minutes, until the mixture is thickened and smooth.
    - Remove the saucepan from the heat and stir in the butter and vanilla extract until the butter is melted and the mixture is well combined.
4. Assemble and Bake:
    - Pour the maple cream filling into the partially baked pie crust, spreading it out evenly.
    - Return the pie to the oven and bake for an additional 25-30 minutes, or until the filling is set and the crust is golden brown.
    - If the crust edges start to darken too quickly, cover them with aluminum foil or a pie crust shield to prevent burning.
5. Cool and Serve:
    - Let the maple cream pie cool completely on a wire rack before serving.
    - Optionally, garnish slices of pie with whipped cream and a drizzle of maple syrup before serving.

Tips:

- Make sure to use pure maple syrup for the best flavor in the filling.
- Be sure to fully cook the filling until it's thickened to avoid a runny pie.

This maple cream pie is a decadent dessert that's perfect for special occasions or anytime you're craving a sweet and indulgent treat. Enjoy the rich, creamy texture and the irresistible flavor of maple in every bite!

Raspberry Fool

Ingredients:

- 2 cups fresh raspberries (or thawed frozen raspberries)
- 1/4 cup granulated sugar, or to taste
- 1 cup heavy cream
- 1/4 cup powdered sugar, or to taste
- 1 teaspoon vanilla extract
- Additional raspberries and mint leaves for garnish (optional)

Instructions:

1. Prepare the Raspberry Puree:
   - In a blender or food processor, puree the raspberries until smooth. If desired, you can strain the puree through a fine-mesh sieve to remove the seeds, although this step is optional.
2. Sweeten the Raspberry Puree:
   - Transfer the raspberry puree to a mixing bowl and stir in the granulated sugar, adjusting the amount to taste. The sweetness will depend on the ripeness of your raspberries and your personal preference. Set aside.
3. Whip the Cream:
   - In a separate mixing bowl, whip the heavy cream, powdered sugar, and vanilla extract together until soft peaks form. Be careful not to over-whip the cream.
4. Fold in the Raspberry Puree:
   - Gently fold the raspberry puree into the whipped cream until evenly combined. Be careful not to overmix, as you want to maintain a marbled effect.
5. Assemble the Raspberry Fool:
   - Spoon the raspberry fool into serving glasses or bowls, layering it with additional dollops of raspberry puree if desired.
   - You can also swirl the raspberry puree through the whipped cream for a marbled effect.
6. Chill and Serve:
   - Cover the raspberry fool and refrigerate for at least 1 hour, or until chilled and set.
   - Serve the raspberry fool cold, garnished with fresh raspberries and mint leaves if desired.

Variations:

- You can use other berries or fruit to make different variations of fool, such as strawberry, blueberry, or mango.
- For added texture, you can fold in crushed meringue or crumbled shortbread cookies into the raspberry fool before chilling.

This raspberry fool is a delightful dessert that's both simple to make and incredibly delicious. Enjoy its light and creamy texture, with the vibrant flavor of fresh raspberries shining through!

Lemon Lush

Ingredients:

For the Crust:

- 1 1/2 cups graham cracker crumbs
- 1/3 cup granulated sugar
- 1/2 cup unsalted butter, melted

For the Lemon Pudding Layer:

- 1 (3.4 oz) package instant lemon pudding mix
- 1 3/4 cups cold milk

For the Whipped Topping:

- 1 cup heavy cream
- 1/4 cup powdered sugar
- 1 teaspoon vanilla extract

Optional Garnish:

- Lemon zest
- Crushed graham crackers or cookies

Instructions:

1. Prepare the Crust:
    - In a mixing bowl, combine the graham cracker crumbs, granulated sugar, and melted butter. Mix until well combined.
    - Press the mixture evenly into the bottom of a 9x13-inch baking dish to form the crust. Use the bottom of a measuring cup or glass to press it down firmly.
    - Place the baking dish in the refrigerator to chill while you prepare the filling.
2. Prepare the Lemon Pudding Layer:
    - In a large mixing bowl, whisk together the instant lemon pudding mix and cold milk until smooth and thickened, about 2 minutes.
    - Spread the lemon pudding evenly over the chilled crust layer. Use a spatula to smooth it out.
3. Prepare the Whipped Topping:

- In another mixing bowl, beat the heavy cream, powdered sugar, and vanilla extract until stiff peaks form.
- Spread the whipped topping over the lemon pudding layer, covering it completely.
4. Chill and Serve:
    - Cover the lemon lush with plastic wrap and refrigerate for at least 4 hours, or until set and chilled.
    - Before serving, optionally garnish with lemon zest and/or crushed graham crackers or cookies for added flavor and texture.
    - Cut into squares and serve chilled.

Tips:

- For a shortcut, you can use store-bought whipped topping instead of making your own.
- Feel free to adjust the sweetness and tartness of the dessert by adding more or less sugar to the lemon pudding layer.
- You can also add a layer of sliced fresh berries (such as strawberries or raspberries) between the lemon pudding and whipped topping layers for a fruity variation.

This lemon lush is a crowd-pleasing dessert that's perfect for potlucks, picnics, or any occasion where you want a refreshing and creamy treat!

Baked Alaska

Ingredients:

For the Cake:

- 1 prepared 9-inch round cake (flavor of your choice), cooled

For the Ice Cream:

- 1 quart (about 4 cups) ice cream, softened (flavor of your choice)

For the Meringue:

- 4 large egg whites, at room temperature
- 1/4 teaspoon cream of tartar
- 1/2 cup granulated sugar
- 1 teaspoon vanilla extract

Instructions:

1. Prepare the Cake:
    - Bake your favorite cake in a 9-inch round cake pan according to the recipe instructions. Allow the cake to cool completely.
2. Prepare the Ice Cream Layer:
    - Line a 9-inch round mixing bowl with plastic wrap, leaving some overhang for easy removal.
    - Spread the softened ice cream evenly into the lined bowl, smoothing the top with a spatula. Cover with plastic wrap and freeze until firm, about 2-3 hours or overnight.
3. Assemble the Baked Alaska:
    - Place the cooled cake on a baking sheet lined with parchment paper or aluminum foil.
    - Invert the bowl of frozen ice cream onto the cake layer, peeling away the plastic wrap.
    - Quickly spread the meringue over the entire cake and ice cream assembly, making sure to seal the edges completely.
4. Prepare the Meringue:
    - In a clean, dry mixing bowl, beat the egg whites and cream of tartar with an electric mixer on medium speed until soft peaks form.

- Gradually add the granulated sugar, one tablespoon at a time, while continuing to beat the egg whites. Beat until stiff, glossy peaks form.
- Beat in the vanilla extract until well combined.

5. Bake the Baked Alaska:
    - Preheat your oven to 500°F (260°C).
    - Place the assembled Baked Alaska in the preheated oven and bake for 3-5 minutes, or until the meringue is lightly browned.
6. Serve:
    - Carefully transfer the Baked Alaska to a serving platter using a large spatula or cake lifter.
    - Slice and serve immediately, as the meringue will begin to soften once it comes out of the oven.

Tips:

- Work quickly when assembling and baking the Baked Alaska to prevent the ice cream from melting too much.
- You can customize the flavor of your Baked Alaska by using different cake flavors and ice cream flavors.
- For a show-stopping presentation, you can also flambe the Baked Alaska by drizzling it with a small amount of liqueur and carefully lighting it on fire just before serving.

Baked Alaska is a stunning dessert that combines warm toasted meringue with cold ice cream and cake, creating a delightful contrast in flavors and textures. Enjoy this classic dessert for a special occasion or anytime you want to impress your guests!

Figgy Duff

Ingredients:

- 2 cups all-purpose flour
- 1 cup fresh breadcrumbs (or use dried breadcrumbs)
- 1 cup granulated sugar
- 1 teaspoon baking soda
- 1/2 teaspoon ground cinnamon
- 1/2 teaspoon ground nutmeg
- 1/2 teaspoon salt
- 1 cup raisins (or dried figs, chopped)
- 1 cup milk
- 1/4 cup molasses
- 1/4 cup butter, melted
- Vanilla sauce or custard, for serving (optional)

Instructions:

1. Prepare the Steamer:
    - If you're using a steamer, fill the bottom with water and bring it to a simmer. Make sure you have a tight-fitting lid.
2. Mix Dry Ingredients:
    - In a large mixing bowl, combine the flour, breadcrumbs, sugar, baking soda, cinnamon, nutmeg, and salt. Stir in the raisins (or dried figs).
3. Add Wet Ingredients:
    - In another bowl, mix together the milk, molasses, and melted butter.
4. Combine Wet and Dry Ingredients:
    - Gradually add the wet ingredients to the dry ingredients, stirring until just combined. Be careful not to overmix.
5. Form the Dough:
    - The dough should be moist but firm enough to hold its shape. If it's too dry, add a little more milk. If it's too wet, add a little more flour.
6. Shape and Steam:
    - Shape the dough into a round loaf or dumpling and place it on a piece of parchment paper or foil.
    - If steaming, place the parchment paper or foil with the dough in the steamer basket. If boiling, wrap the dough securely in the parchment paper or foil.

- Steam or boil the Figgy Duff for about 2 hours, or until firm and cooked through. Check the water level periodically and add more boiling water if necessary.

7. **Serve:**
    - Carefully remove the Figgy Duff from the steamer or pot and let it cool for a few minutes.
    - Slice and serve warm with vanilla sauce or custard, if desired.

Tips:

- You can customize the recipe by adding other dried fruits or nuts, such as chopped dates, currants, or walnuts.
- Figgy Duff can also be baked in the oven if you prefer. Simply place the dough in a greased baking dish, cover with foil, and bake at 350°F (175°C) for about 1 hour, or until cooked through.

Enjoy this comforting and nostalgic Newfoundland dessert with a cup of tea or coffee for a cozy and delicious treat!

Maple Pecan Squares

Ingredients:

For the Crust:

- 1 1/2 cups all-purpose flour
- 1/2 cup unsalted butter, cold and cubed
- 1/4 cup granulated sugar
- 1/4 teaspoon salt

For the Maple Pecan Filling:

- 3/4 cup pure maple syrup
- 1/2 cup packed brown sugar
- 2 large eggs
- 2 tablespoons all-purpose flour
- 1/4 teaspoon salt
- 1 teaspoon vanilla extract
- 1 cup chopped pecans

Instructions:

1. Preheat the Oven:
    - Preheat your oven to 350°F (175°C). Grease or line an 8x8-inch baking pan with parchment paper.
2. Prepare the Crust:
    - In a food processor or mixing bowl, combine the flour, cold cubed butter, granulated sugar, and salt.
    - Pulse or mix until the mixture resembles coarse crumbs and starts to come together.
    - Press the mixture firmly into the bottom of the prepared baking pan to form an even crust.
3. Bake the Crust:
    - Bake the crust in the preheated oven for 15-20 minutes, or until lightly golden brown.
4. Prepare the Maple Pecan Filling:
    - In a medium bowl, whisk together the pure maple syrup, brown sugar, eggs, flour, salt, and vanilla extract until smooth.
    - Stir in the chopped pecans until evenly distributed.

5. Assemble and Bake:
    - Pour the maple pecan filling over the partially baked crust, spreading it out evenly.
6. Bake:
    - Return the baking pan to the oven and bake for an additional 25-30 minutes, or until the filling is set and the edges are golden brown.
7. Cool and Serve:
    - Allow the maple pecan squares to cool completely in the baking pan on a wire rack.
    - Once cooled, slice into squares or bars.
8. Optional: Garnish:
    - Optionally, you can dust the maple pecan squares with powdered sugar before serving for a decorative touch.

Tips:

- Make sure to let the squares cool completely before slicing to allow the filling to set properly.
- Store any leftovers in an airtight container at room temperature for up to 3 days, or refrigerate for longer storage.

These maple pecan squares are perfect for enjoying as a sweet treat with a cup of coffee or tea, or as a delicious dessert for any occasion. Enjoy the wonderful combination of maple syrup, pecans, and buttery crust in every bite!

Sour Cream Pound Cake

Ingredients:

- 1 cup unsalted butter, softened
- 3 cups granulated sugar
- 6 large eggs, at room temperature
- 1 cup full-fat sour cream
- 1 teaspoon vanilla extract
- 3 cups all-purpose flour
- 1/4 teaspoon baking soda
- 1/4 teaspoon salt

Instructions:

1. Preheat the Oven:
    - Preheat your oven to 325°F (160°C). Grease and flour a 10-inch tube or bundt pan.
2. Cream the Butter and Sugar:
    - In a large mixing bowl, cream together the softened butter and granulated sugar until light and fluffy, about 3-4 minutes.
3. Add Eggs and Sour Cream:
    - Add the eggs one at a time, beating well after each addition.
    - Mix in the sour cream and vanilla extract until well combined.
4. Mix Dry Ingredients:
    - In a separate bowl, whisk together the flour, baking soda, and salt.
5. Incorporate Dry Ingredients:
    - Gradually add the dry ingredients to the wet ingredients, mixing until just combined. Be careful not to overmix.
6. Bake:
    - Pour the batter into the prepared tube or bundt pan, spreading it out evenly.
    - Bake in the preheated oven for 1 hour and 15 minutes to 1 hour and 30 minutes, or until a toothpick inserted into the center comes out clean.
7. Cool:
    - Allow the pound cake to cool in the pan for about 15 minutes before transferring it to a wire rack to cool completely.
8. Serve:

- Once cooled, slice the sour cream pound cake and serve it plain or with your favorite toppings, such as whipped cream, fresh berries, or a dusting of powdered sugar.

Tips:

- Make sure your ingredients are at room temperature to ensure proper incorporation and a smooth batter.
- You can customize the flavor of the pound cake by adding lemon zest or almond extract for a citrus or nutty twist.
- Store any leftovers in an airtight container at room temperature for up to 3 days, or in the refrigerator for longer storage.

This sour cream pound cake is a timeless dessert that's sure to impress with its moist and tender crumb and buttery flavor. Enjoy it for any occasion, from afternoon tea to special celebrations!

Canadian Sugar Pie

Ingredients:

For the Pie Crust:

- 1 9-inch pie crust (store-bought or homemade)

For the Sugar Filling:

- 1 cup packed brown sugar
- 1/4 cup all-purpose flour
- 1/4 teaspoon salt
- 1 cup heavy cream
- 1/4 cup unsalted butter, melted
- 1 teaspoon vanilla extract

Instructions:

1. Preheat the Oven:
   - Preheat your oven to 350°F (175°C). Place the pie crust in a 9-inch pie plate and set aside.
2. Prepare the Sugar Filling:
   - In a medium mixing bowl, whisk together the packed brown sugar, flour, and salt until well combined.
   - Gradually whisk in the heavy cream until smooth.
   - Stir in the melted butter and vanilla extract until evenly incorporated.
3. Assemble and Bake:
   - Pour the sugar filling into the prepared pie crust, spreading it out evenly.
4. Bake:
   - Place the pie in the preheated oven and bake for 35-40 minutes, or until the filling is set and golden brown on top. The center may still jiggle slightly when gently shaken, but it will firm up as it cools.
5. Cool and Serve:
   - Allow the Canadian sugar pie to cool completely on a wire rack before serving.
   - Once cooled, slice the pie into wedges and serve at room temperature or slightly warmed.

Tips:

- You can make the pie crust from scratch using your favorite recipe or use a store-bought crust for convenience.
- For added flavor, you can sprinkle the top of the pie with a little extra brown sugar before baking.
- Serve the sugar pie with a dollop of whipped cream or a scoop of vanilla ice cream for a deliciously indulgent treat.

This Canadian sugar pie is a comforting and satisfying dessert that's perfect for enjoying on a chilly day or as a sweet ending to any meal. Enjoy the rich, caramelized flavor of this classic Canadian treat!

Black Forest Cake

Ingredients:

For the Chocolate Cake Layers:

- 1 3/4 cups all-purpose flour
- 3/4 cup unsweetened cocoa powder
- 2 cups granulated sugar
- 2 teaspoons baking soda
- 1 teaspoon baking powder
- 1 teaspoon salt
- 2 large eggs, at room temperature
- 1 cup buttermilk, at room temperature
- 1/2 cup vegetable oil
- 2 teaspoons vanilla extract
- 1 cup hot water

For the Filling and Topping:

- 2 (14-ounce) cans pitted cherries in juice, drained (reserve the juice)
- 2 tablespoons cornstarch
- 1/4 cup granulated sugar
- 2 cups heavy cream, chilled
- 1/4 cup powdered sugar
- 1 teaspoon vanilla extract
- Chocolate shavings or curls, for garnish (optional)
- Maraschino cherries, for garnish (optional)

Instructions:

1. Preheat the Oven:
    - Preheat your oven to 350°F (175°C). Grease and flour two 9-inch round cake pans.
2. Prepare the Chocolate Cake Layers:
    - In a large mixing bowl, sift together the flour, cocoa powder, granulated sugar, baking soda, baking powder, and salt.
    - Add the eggs, buttermilk, vegetable oil, and vanilla extract to the dry ingredients. Beat on medium speed until well combined.
    - Stir in the hot water until the batter is smooth. The batter will be thin.

- Divide the batter evenly between the prepared cake pans.
3. Bake the Cake Layers:
    - Bake in the preheated oven for 30-35 minutes, or until a toothpick inserted into the center of the cakes comes out clean.
    - Remove the cakes from the oven and let them cool in the pans for 10 minutes before transferring them to wire racks to cool completely.
4. Prepare the Cherry Filling:
    - In a small saucepan, combine the drained cherries, reserved cherry juice, cornstarch, and granulated sugar.
    - Cook over medium heat, stirring constantly, until the mixture thickens and comes to a simmer. Remove from heat and let it cool completely.
5. Make the Whipped Cream:
    - In a large mixing bowl, beat the chilled heavy cream, powdered sugar, and vanilla extract until stiff peaks form.
6. Assemble the Cake:
    - Place one of the cooled chocolate cake layers on a serving platter. Spread half of the whipped cream over the top.
    - Spoon half of the cooled cherry filling over the whipped cream.
    - Top with the second chocolate cake layer. Spread the remaining whipped cream over the top.
    - Spoon the remaining cherry filling over the whipped cream.
    - Garnish the cake with chocolate shavings or curls and maraschino cherries, if desired.
7. Chill and Serve:
    - Refrigerate the Black Forest cake for at least 1 hour before serving to allow the flavors to meld together.
    - Slice and serve chilled.

Tips:

- For an extra indulgent touch, you can brush the chocolate cake layers with a little cherry liqueur before assembling the cake.
- To make chocolate shavings or curls, use a vegetable peeler to shave a block of chocolate.
- Store any leftover cake in the refrigerator. It's best enjoyed within a few days.

This Black Forest cake is sure to impress with its rich chocolate layers, fluffy whipped cream, and sweet cherries. Enjoy this decadent dessert for special occasions or anytime you're craving something deliciously indulgent!

Plum Pudding

Ingredients:

- 1 cup raisins
- 1 cup currants
- 1 cup chopped dried figs
- 1 cup chopped dates
- 1/2 cup chopped candied peel (optional)
- 1/2 cup chopped almonds or walnuts
- 1/2 cup brandy or rum
- Zest of 1 lemon
- Zest of 1 orange
- 1 cup all-purpose flour
- 1 cup fresh breadcrumbs
- 1 cup suet (or vegetable shortening for a vegetarian version)
- 1 cup dark brown sugar
- 1 teaspoon ground cinnamon
- 1/2 teaspoon ground nutmeg
- 1/4 teaspoon ground cloves
- 4 large eggs, beaten
- 1/2 cup milk

Instructions:

1. Prepare the Fruit Mixture:
    - In a large mixing bowl, combine the raisins, currants, chopped figs, dates, candied peel (if using), chopped nuts, brandy or rum, lemon zest, and orange zest. Mix well to combine. Cover and let the mixture soak overnight, or for at least 8 hours.
2. Prepare the Pudding Batter:
    - In a separate large mixing bowl, combine the flour, breadcrumbs, suet or vegetable shortening, brown sugar, cinnamon, nutmeg, and cloves. Mix well to combine.
    - Stir in the beaten eggs and milk until the batter is smooth.
3. Combine the Fruit Mixture and Batter:
    - Gradually add the soaked fruit mixture to the pudding batter, stirring until evenly distributed.
4. Prepare the Pudding Basin:

- Grease a 2-quart pudding basin or heatproof bowl with butter. Place a small round of parchment paper on the bottom to prevent sticking.
5. Fill the Pudding Basin:
    - Spoon the pudding mixture into the prepared basin, pressing it down lightly and smoothing the top with the back of a spoon.
6. Steam the Pudding:
    - Cover the pudding basin tightly with a double layer of greased parchment paper or foil, securing it with kitchen twine.
    - Place the basin in a large pot and pour boiling water into the pot until it reaches halfway up the sides of the basin.
    - Cover the pot with a tight-fitting lid and steam the pudding over low heat for about 6 hours, adding more boiling water as needed to maintain the water level.
7. Cool and Store:
    - Once steamed, remove the pudding basin from the pot and let it cool for a few minutes before unmolding.
    - Allow the plum pudding to cool completely before wrapping it tightly in plastic wrap and storing it in a cool, dark place for at least a few weeks to allow the flavors to develop.
8. Serve:
    - To serve, reheat the plum pudding by steaming it for 2-3 hours. Serve with brandy sauce, custard, or whipped cream.

Tips:

- Make sure to use fresh breadcrumbs for the best texture.
- If you prefer, you can substitute the brandy or rum with apple juice.
- You can make the pudding several weeks in advance, as it improves with age. Reheat it before serving as directed.

Enjoy this traditional plum pudding as a festive and comforting dessert during the holiday season!

Maple Pecan Pie

Ingredients:

For the Pie Crust:

- 1 9-inch unbaked pie crust (store-bought or homemade)

For the Maple Pecan Filling:

- 1 cup pure maple syrup
- 3/4 cup packed brown sugar
- 3 large eggs
- 1/4 cup unsalted butter, melted
- 1 teaspoon vanilla extract
- 1/4 teaspoon salt
- 1 1/2 cups pecan halves

Instructions:

1. Preheat the Oven:
    - Preheat your oven to 375°F (190°C).
2. Prepare the Pie Crust:
    - Line a 9-inch pie plate with the unbaked pie crust. Crimp the edges as desired. Prick the bottom of the crust with a fork to prevent bubbling during baking.
    - Place the pie crust in the refrigerator while you prepare the filling.
3. Prepare the Maple Pecan Filling:
    - In a large mixing bowl, whisk together the pure maple syrup, brown sugar, eggs, melted butter, vanilla extract, and salt until well combined.
    - Stir in the pecan halves until evenly coated.
4. Assemble and Bake:
    - Pour the maple pecan filling into the prepared pie crust, spreading it out evenly.
5. Bake:
    - Place the pie in the preheated oven and bake for 40-50 minutes, or until the filling is set and the crust is golden brown.
    - If the crust edges start to darken too quickly, cover them with aluminum foil or a pie crust shield to prevent burning.
6. Cool and Serve:

- Allow the maple pecan pie to cool completely on a wire rack before serving.
- Once cooled, slice into wedges and serve at room temperature or slightly warmed.

Tips:

- Make sure to use pure maple syrup for the best flavor in the filling.
- You can lightly toast the pecans before adding them to the filling for extra flavor.
- Serve the pie with a dollop of whipped cream or a scoop of vanilla ice cream for a delicious finishing touch.

This maple pecan pie is a decadent and irresistible dessert that's perfect for holidays, special occasions, or anytime you're craving a sweet treat with a delightful maple twist!

Butter Pecan Ice Cream

Ingredients:

- 1 cup pecan halves
- 4 tablespoons unsalted butter
- 2 cups heavy cream
- 1 cup whole milk
- 3/4 cup granulated sugar
- Pinch of salt
- 5 large egg yolks
- 1 teaspoon vanilla extract

Instructions:

1. Toast the Pecans:
    - Preheat your oven to 350°F (175°C). Spread the pecan halves in a single layer on a baking sheet.
    - Toast the pecans in the preheated oven for 8-10 minutes, or until fragrant and lightly browned. Watch them carefully to prevent burning. Once toasted, remove from the oven and let them cool completely. Chop the pecans into smaller pieces.
2. Prepare the Butter Pecan Mixture:
    - In a medium saucepan, melt the butter over medium heat. Add the chopped pecans and cook, stirring frequently, for 3-4 minutes, or until the pecans are toasted and coated with butter. Remove from heat and set aside.
3. Prepare the Ice Cream Base:
    - In a separate saucepan, heat the heavy cream, whole milk, granulated sugar, and a pinch of salt over medium heat. Stir occasionally until the mixture reaches a simmer. Do not boil.
    - In a mixing bowl, whisk the egg yolks until smooth. Slowly pour about 1/2 cup of the hot cream mixture into the egg yolks, whisking constantly to temper the yolks.
    - Pour the tempered egg mixture back into the saucepan with the remaining cream mixture, stirring constantly.
    - Cook the mixture over medium heat, stirring constantly with a wooden spoon, until it thickens slightly and coats the back of the spoon, about 5-7 minutes. Do not let it boil.

- Remove the saucepan from the heat and strain the mixture through a fine-mesh sieve into a clean bowl. Discard any solids.
4. Chill the Mixture:
    - Place the bowl with the ice cream base in an ice bath or refrigerator until completely chilled, about 2-3 hours or overnight.
5. Churn the Ice Cream:
    - Once the mixture is chilled, pour it into an ice cream maker and churn according to the manufacturer's instructions until it reaches a soft-serve consistency.
6. Add Pecans:
    - During the last few minutes of churning, add the toasted butter pecans to the ice cream maker and continue churning until evenly distributed.
7. Freeze:
    - Transfer the churned ice cream to a freezer-safe container, smoothing the top with a spatula.
    - Cover the container with a lid or plastic wrap and freeze the ice cream for at least 4 hours, or until firm.
8. Serve:
    - Once the butter pecan ice cream is fully frozen, scoop it into bowls or cones and enjoy!

Tips:

- For a more intense butter pecan flavor, you can brown the butter before adding the pecans.
- For extra texture, you can reserve a portion of the toasted pecans to add to the churned ice cream just before freezing.
- Store any leftover ice cream in an airtight container in the freezer for up to two weeks.

Enjoy this creamy, buttery treat with crunchy pecans as a delightful dessert on its own or alongside your favorite pie or cake!

Maple Oatmeal Cookies

Ingredients:

- 1 cup (2 sticks) unsalted butter, softened
- 1 cup packed light brown sugar
- 1/2 cup granulated sugar
- 2 large eggs
- 1 teaspoon vanilla extract
- 1/2 cup pure maple syrup
- 1 1/2 cups all-purpose flour
- 1 teaspoon baking soda
- 1 teaspoon ground cinnamon
- 1/2 teaspoon salt
- 3 cups old-fashioned rolled oats
- Optional: 1 cup chopped nuts (such as walnuts or pecans), chocolate chips, or dried fruit (such as raisins or cranberries)

Instructions:

1. Preheat the Oven:
    - Preheat your oven to 350°F (175°C). Line baking sheets with parchment paper or silicone baking mats.
2. Cream the Butter and Sugars:
    - In a large mixing bowl, cream together the softened butter, brown sugar, and granulated sugar until light and fluffy.
3. Add Wet Ingredients:
    - Beat in the eggs one at a time, followed by the vanilla extract and maple syrup, until well combined.
4. Combine Dry Ingredients:
    - In a separate bowl, whisk together the flour, baking soda, cinnamon, and salt.
5. Incorporate Dry Ingredients:
    - Gradually add the dry ingredients to the wet ingredients, mixing until just combined.
6. Add Oats (and Optional Ingredients):
    - Stir in the rolled oats until evenly distributed. If using, fold in the chopped nuts, chocolate chips, or dried fruit.
7. Scoop and Bake:

- Drop rounded tablespoons of cookie dough onto the prepared baking sheets, spacing them about 2 inches apart.
    - Flatten the dough slightly with the back of a spoon or your fingers.
8. Bake:
    - Bake in the preheated oven for 10-12 minutes, or until the edges are lightly golden brown.
9. Cool and Serve:
    - Allow the cookies to cool on the baking sheets for a few minutes before transferring them to wire racks to cool completely.
    - Once cooled, store the cookies in an airtight container at room temperature for up to one week.

Tips:

- For chewier cookies, slightly underbake them and let them cool completely on the baking sheet before transferring them to a wire rack.
- Feel free to customize these cookies with your favorite mix-ins, such as chopped nuts, chocolate chips, or dried fruit.
- If you prefer a stronger maple flavor, you can add a few drops of maple extract to the dough along with the vanilla extract.

Enjoy these maple oatmeal cookies with a glass of milk or a cup of tea for a cozy and delicious treat!

Raspberry Pie

Ingredients:

For the Pie Crust:

- 2 1/2 cups all-purpose flour
- 1 teaspoon salt
- 1 tablespoon granulated sugar
- 1 cup unsalted butter, cold and cubed
- 1/4 to 1/2 cup ice water

For the Raspberry Filling:

- 6 cups fresh raspberries
- 3/4 cup granulated sugar (adjust to taste depending on sweetness of raspberries)
- 1/4 cup cornstarch
- 1 tablespoon lemon juice
- Zest of 1 lemon
- 1 teaspoon vanilla extract
- 2 tablespoons unsalted butter, cut into small pieces

For Assembly:

- 1 egg, beaten (for egg wash)
- Granulated sugar, for sprinkling (optional)

Instructions:

1. Prepare the Pie Crust:
    - In a large mixing bowl, combine the flour, salt, and granulated sugar.
    - Add the cold cubed butter and use a pastry cutter or your fingers to cut the butter into the flour mixture until it resembles coarse crumbs with some pea-sized pieces.
    - Gradually add the ice water, a tablespoon at a time, mixing until the dough just begins to come together. Be careful not to overwork the dough.
    - Divide the dough into two equal portions, shape each into a disc, wrap in plastic wrap, and refrigerate for at least 1 hour, or until firm.
2. Prepare the Raspberry Filling:

- In a large mixing bowl, gently toss together the fresh raspberries, granulated sugar, cornstarch, lemon juice, lemon zest, and vanilla extract until well combined. Set aside.
3. Preheat the Oven:
    - Preheat your oven to 400°F (200°C). Place a baking sheet in the oven to preheat as well.
4. Roll Out the Pie Crust:
    - On a lightly floured surface, roll out one disc of chilled pie dough into a circle about 12 inches in diameter. Carefully transfer it to a 9-inch pie dish, gently pressing it into the bottom and up the sides.
5. Fill the Pie:
    - Spoon the raspberry filling into the prepared pie crust, spreading it out evenly. Dot the top with small pieces of butter.
6. Top and Seal the Pie:
    - Roll out the second disc of chilled pie dough into a circle about 12 inches in diameter. Place it over the filling.
    - Trim any excess dough from the edges and crimp the edges of the pie crust to seal. Cut a few slits in the top crust to allow steam to escape.
7. Bake the Pie:
    - Brush the top crust with the beaten egg and sprinkle with granulated sugar, if desired.
    - Place the pie on the preheated baking sheet and bake for 45-55 minutes, or until the crust is golden brown and the filling is bubbly.
8. Cool and Serve:
    - Allow the raspberry pie to cool on a wire rack for at least 2 hours before serving to allow the filling to set. Serve slices of pie with a scoop of vanilla ice cream or whipped cream, if desired.

Tips:

- If the edges of the pie crust start to brown too quickly during baking, cover them loosely with aluminum foil to prevent burning.
- You can use frozen raspberries instead of fresh ones, but be sure to thaw and drain them before using to prevent excess liquid in the filling.
- Feel free to add other berries or fruits to the filling for a mixed berry pie variation.

Enjoy this delicious homemade raspberry pie as a sweet and tangy dessert that's perfect for any occasion!

Maple Glazed Donuts

Ingredients:

For the Donuts:

- 2 1/4 teaspoons (1 packet) active dry yeast
- 1/4 cup warm water (about 110°F or 45°C)
- 3/4 cup warm milk (about 110°F or 45°C)
- 1/4 cup granulated sugar
- 1 teaspoon salt
- 1/4 cup unsalted butter, melted
- 2 large eggs
- 4 cups all-purpose flour
- Vegetable oil, for frying

For the Maple Glaze:

- 2 cups confectioners' sugar
- 1/4 cup pure maple syrup
- 1/4 cup milk (adjust as needed for desired consistency)
- 1 teaspoon vanilla extract

Instructions:

1. Activate the Yeast:
    - In a small bowl, dissolve the active dry yeast in warm water. Let it sit for 5-10 minutes until frothy.
2. Make the Dough:
    - In a large mixing bowl or the bowl of a stand mixer fitted with the dough hook attachment, combine the warm milk, granulated sugar, salt, melted butter, eggs, and activated yeast mixture.
    - Gradually add the flour, mixing until a soft dough forms. Knead the dough for about 5 minutes until smooth and elastic.
3. First Rise:
    - Place the dough in a greased bowl, cover with a clean kitchen towel or plastic wrap, and let it rise in a warm, draft-free place for 1-2 hours, or until doubled in size.
4. Shape the Donuts:

- After the dough has risen, punch it down and transfer it to a lightly floured surface. Roll out the dough to about 1/2 inch thickness.
- Using a donut cutter or two differently sized round cookie cutters, cut out donuts and donut holes. Re-roll any scraps and repeat until all the dough is used.
- Place the cut-out donuts and holes on a lightly floured baking sheet, cover with a clean kitchen towel, and let them rise for another 30-45 minutes.

5. Fry the Donuts:
   - Heat vegetable oil in a deep fryer or large pot to 350°F (175°C). Carefully add the donuts to the hot oil, a few at a time, and fry for 1-2 minutes per side until golden brown.
   - Use a slotted spoon or spider strainer to remove the donuts from the oil and transfer them to a wire rack set over paper towels to drain and cool.
6. Make the Maple Glaze:
   - In a medium bowl, whisk together the confectioners' sugar, maple syrup, milk, and vanilla extract until smooth and well combined.
7. Glaze the Donuts:
   - Dip each cooled donut into the maple glaze, allowing any excess glaze to drip off. Place the glazed donuts back on the wire rack to set.
8. Serve:
   - Serve the maple glazed donuts immediately, or store them in an airtight container for up to 2 days.

Tips:

- For a richer flavor, you can add a pinch of cinnamon or nutmeg to the donut dough.
- Be sure to fry the donuts in batches, being careful not to overcrowd the fryer or pot.
- You can sprinkle chopped nuts, toasted coconut, or bacon bits on top of the glaze for extra flavor and texture.

Enjoy these homemade maple glazed donuts with a cup of coffee or hot cocoa for a delicious breakfast or snack!

Saskatoon Berry Crisp

Ingredients:

For the Saskatoon Berry Filling:

- 6 cups fresh Saskatoon berries, washed and drained (or frozen berries, thawed and drained)
- 1/2 cup granulated sugar (adjust to taste depending on sweetness of berries)
- 2 tablespoons all-purpose flour
- 1 tablespoon lemon juice
- Zest of 1 lemon
- 1 teaspoon vanilla extract

For the Oat Topping:

- 1 cup old-fashioned rolled oats
- 1/2 cup all-purpose flour
- 1/2 cup packed light brown sugar
- 1/4 teaspoon ground cinnamon
- 1/4 teaspoon salt
- 1/2 cup unsalted butter, melted

Instructions:

1. Preheat the Oven:
    - Preheat your oven to 350°F (175°C). Grease a 9x9-inch baking dish or a similar-sized dish.
2. Prepare the Saskatoon Berry Filling:
    - In a large mixing bowl, gently toss together the Saskatoon berries, granulated sugar, all-purpose flour, lemon juice, lemon zest, and vanilla extract until well combined. Transfer the mixture to the prepared baking dish, spreading it out evenly.
3. Make the Oat Topping:
    - In another mixing bowl, combine the rolled oats, all-purpose flour, brown sugar, ground cinnamon, and salt.
    - Pour the melted butter over the oat mixture and stir until the ingredients are evenly moistened and crumbly.
4. Assemble and Bake:

- Sprinkle the oat topping evenly over the Saskatoon berry filling in the baking dish, covering it completely.
5. Bake the Crisp:
    - Place the baking dish in the preheated oven and bake for 35-40 minutes, or until the filling is bubbly and the topping is golden brown.
6. Cool and Serve:
    - Remove the Saskatoon berry crisp from the oven and let it cool for a few minutes before serving.
    - Serve warm with a scoop of vanilla ice cream or a dollop of whipped cream, if desired.

Tips:

- If you prefer a thicker filling, you can increase the amount of flour in the Saskatoon berry mixture.
- You can customize the oat topping by adding chopped nuts, such as almonds or pecans, for extra crunch and flavor.
- Leftover crisp can be stored in an airtight container in the refrigerator for up to 3 days. Reheat in the oven or microwave before serving.

Enjoy this delicious Saskatoon berry crisp as a comforting dessert that highlights the natural sweetness of Saskatoon berries!

Wild Blueberry Pie

Ingredients:

For the Pie Crust:

- 2 1/2 cups all-purpose flour
- 1 teaspoon salt
- 1 tablespoon granulated sugar
- 1 cup unsalted butter, cold and cubed
- 1/4 to 1/2 cup ice water

For the Blueberry Filling:

- 6 cups fresh or frozen wild blueberries
- 3/4 cup granulated sugar (adjust to taste depending on sweetness of blueberries)
- 1/4 cup cornstarch
- 1 tablespoon lemon juice
- Zest of 1 lemon
- 1 teaspoon vanilla extract
- 2 tablespoons unsalted butter, cut into small pieces

Instructions:

1. Prepare the Pie Crust:
    - In a large mixing bowl, combine the flour, salt, and granulated sugar.
    - Add the cold cubed butter and use a pastry cutter or your fingers to cut the butter into the flour mixture until it resembles coarse crumbs with some pea-sized pieces.
    - Gradually add the ice water, a tablespoon at a time, mixing until the dough just begins to come together. Be careful not to overwork the dough.
    - Divide the dough into two equal portions, shape each into a disc, wrap in plastic wrap, and refrigerate for at least 1 hour, or until firm.
2. Prepare the Blueberry Filling:
    - In a large mixing bowl, gently toss together the wild blueberries, granulated sugar, cornstarch, lemon juice, lemon zest, and vanilla extract until well combined. Set aside.
3. Preheat the Oven:

- Preheat your oven to 400°F (200°C). Place a baking sheet in the oven to preheat as well.
4. Roll Out the Pie Crust:
    - On a lightly floured surface, roll out one disc of chilled pie dough into a circle about 12 inches in diameter. Carefully transfer it to a 9-inch pie dish, gently pressing it into the bottom and up the sides.
5. Fill the Pie:
    - Spoon the blueberry filling into the prepared pie crust, spreading it out evenly. Dot the top with small pieces of butter.
6. Top and Seal the Pie:
    - Roll out the second disc of chilled pie dough into a circle about 12 inches in diameter. Place it over the filling.
    - Trim any excess dough from the edges and crimp the edges of the pie crust to seal. Cut a few slits in the top crust to allow steam to escape.
7. Bake the Pie:
    - Place the pie on the preheated baking sheet and bake for 45-55 minutes, or until the crust is golden brown and the filling is bubbly.
8. Cool and Serve:
    - Allow the wild blueberry pie to cool on a wire rack for at least 2 hours before serving to allow the filling to set. Serve slices of pie with a scoop of vanilla ice cream or whipped cream, if desired.

Tips:

- If the edges of the pie crust start to brown too quickly during baking, cover them loosely with aluminum foil to prevent burning.
- You can use frozen wild blueberries instead of fresh ones, but be sure to thaw and drain them before using to prevent excess liquid in the filling.
- Feel free to add a sprinkle of cinnamon or nutmeg to the blueberry filling for extra flavor.

Enjoy this delicious homemade wild blueberry pie as a sweet and fruity dessert that's perfect for any occasion!

Carrot Cake

Ingredients:

For the Carrot Cake:

- 2 cups all-purpose flour
- 2 teaspoons baking powder
- 1 1/2 teaspoons baking soda
- 1 teaspoon ground cinnamon
- 1/2 teaspoon ground nutmeg
- 1/2 teaspoon ground ginger
- 1/2 teaspoon salt
- 1 cup granulated sugar
- 1 cup packed light brown sugar
- 1 cup vegetable oil
- 4 large eggs
- 2 teaspoons vanilla extract
- 3 cups grated carrots (about 4-5 medium carrots)
- 1 cup chopped walnuts or pecans (optional)
- 1/2 cup crushed pineapple, drained (optional)

For the Cream Cheese Frosting:

- 8 ounces cream cheese, softened
- 1/2 cup unsalted butter, softened
- 4 cups confectioners' sugar
- 1 teaspoon vanilla extract
- Pinch of salt

Instructions:

1. Preheat the Oven:
   - Preheat your oven to 350°F (175°C). Grease and flour two 9-inch round cake pans or one 9x13-inch rectangular cake pan.
2. Prepare the Carrot Cake Batter:
   - In a large mixing bowl, whisk together the flour, baking powder, baking soda, cinnamon, nutmeg, ginger, and salt until well combined.
   - In another large mixing bowl, whisk together the granulated sugar, brown sugar, vegetable oil, eggs, and vanilla extract until smooth.

- Gradually add the dry ingredients to the wet ingredients, mixing until just combined.
- Fold in the grated carrots, chopped nuts (if using), and crushed pineapple (if using) until evenly distributed.

3. Bake the Carrot Cake:
   - Pour the batter into the prepared cake pans, spreading it out evenly.
   - Bake in the preheated oven for 25-30 minutes for round cake pans or 35-40 minutes for a rectangular cake pan, or until a toothpick inserted into the center comes out clean.
   - Remove the cakes from the oven and let them cool in the pans for 10 minutes before transferring them to wire racks to cool completely.
4. Prepare the Cream Cheese Frosting:
   - In a large mixing bowl, beat the softened cream cheese and butter together until smooth and creamy.
   - Gradually add the confectioners' sugar, vanilla extract, and salt, beating until light and fluffy.
5. Assemble the Carrot Cake:
   - Once the cakes are completely cooled, place one layer on a serving plate or cake stand. Spread a layer of cream cheese frosting over the top.
   - Place the second layer on top and spread the remaining frosting over the top and sides of the cake.
   - Optionally, decorate the top of the cake with chopped nuts or additional grated carrots.
6. Chill and Serve:
   - Chill the carrot cake in the refrigerator for at least 1 hour before serving to allow the frosting to set.
   - Slice and serve the carrot cake chilled or at room temperature.

Tips:

- For best results, use freshly grated carrots instead of pre-shredded ones.
- If you prefer a lighter frosting, you can reduce the amount of confectioners' sugar in the cream cheese frosting.
- Store any leftover carrot cake in an airtight container in the refrigerator for up to 5 days.

Enjoy this homemade carrot cake with its creamy frosting as a delightful dessert for any occasion!

Pecan Pie

Ingredients:

For the Pie Crust:

- 1 1/4 cups all-purpose flour
- 1/2 teaspoon salt
- 1/2 teaspoon granulated sugar
- 1/2 cup unsalted butter, cold and cubed
- 3 to 4 tablespoons ice water

For the Pecan Pie Filling:

- 1 cup granulated sugar
- 3/4 cup light corn syrup
- 1/4 cup unsalted butter, melted and cooled slightly
- 3 large eggs
- 1 teaspoon vanilla extract
- 1/4 teaspoon salt
- 1 1/2 cups pecan halves

Instructions:

1. Prepare the Pie Crust:
    - In a large mixing bowl, whisk together the flour, salt, and granulated sugar.
    - Add the cold cubed butter and use a pastry cutter or your fingers to cut the butter into the flour mixture until it resembles coarse crumbs with some pea-sized pieces.
    - Gradually add the ice water, a tablespoon at a time, mixing until the dough just begins to come together. Be careful not to overwork the dough.
    - Shape the dough into a disc, wrap in plastic wrap, and refrigerate for at least 1 hour, or until firm.
2. Preheat the Oven:
    - Preheat your oven to 375°F (190°C).
3. Roll Out the Pie Crust:
    - On a lightly floured surface, roll out the chilled pie crust into a circle about 12 inches in diameter. Carefully transfer it to a 9-inch pie dish, gently pressing it into the bottom and up the sides. Trim any excess dough and crimp the edges as desired.

4. Prepare the Pecan Pie Filling:
   - In a large mixing bowl, whisk together the granulated sugar, light corn syrup, melted butter, eggs, vanilla extract, and salt until well combined.
   - Stir in the pecan halves until evenly coated.
5. Assemble and Bake the Pie:
   - Pour the pecan pie filling into the prepared pie crust, spreading it out evenly.
6. Bake the Pie:
   - Place the pie in the preheated oven and bake for 40-50 minutes, or until the filling is set and the crust is golden brown. If the edges of the crust start to brown too quickly, cover them loosely with aluminum foil.
7. Cool and Serve:
   - Allow the pecan pie to cool completely on a wire rack before slicing and serving. Serve slices of pie with a dollop of whipped cream or a scoop of vanilla ice cream, if desired.

Tips:

- For a deeper flavor, you can toast the pecans in a dry skillet over medium heat for a few minutes before adding them to the filling.
- If you prefer a deeper caramel flavor, you can use dark corn syrup instead of light corn syrup.
- Store any leftover pecan pie in an airtight container in the refrigerator for up to 3 days.

Enjoy this homemade pecan pie as a decadent dessert that's perfect for holidays, special occasions, or anytime you're craving a sweet treat!

Strawberry Rhubarb Pie

Ingredients:

For the Pie Crust:

- 2 1/2 cups all-purpose flour
- 1 teaspoon salt
- 1 tablespoon granulated sugar
- 1 cup unsalted butter, cold and cubed
- 6-8 tablespoons ice water

For the Strawberry Rhubarb Filling:

- 3 cups sliced rhubarb (about 1/2-inch thick)
- 3 cups sliced strawberries
- 1 cup granulated sugar (adjust to taste depending on sweetness of fruit)
- 1/4 cup cornstarch
- 1 tablespoon lemon juice
- 1 teaspoon vanilla extract
- 1/2 teaspoon ground cinnamon
- 1/4 teaspoon ground nutmeg
- 2 tablespoons unsalted butter, cut into small pieces

For Assembly:

- 1 egg, beaten (for egg wash)
- Granulated sugar, for sprinkling (optional)

Instructions:

1. Prepare the Pie Crust:
    - In a large mixing bowl, whisk together the flour, salt, and granulated sugar.
    - Add the cold cubed butter and use a pastry cutter or your fingers to cut the butter into the flour mixture until it resembles coarse crumbs with some pea-sized pieces.
    - Gradually add the ice water, a tablespoon at a time, mixing until the dough just begins to come together. Be careful not to overwork the dough.
    - Divide the dough into two equal portions, shape each into a disc, wrap in plastic wrap, and refrigerate for at least 1 hour, or until firm.
2. Preheat the Oven:

- Preheat your oven to 400°F (200°C). Place a baking sheet in the oven to preheat as well.
3. Prepare the Strawberry Rhubarb Filling:
    - In a large mixing bowl, gently toss together the sliced rhubarb, sliced strawberries, granulated sugar, cornstarch, lemon juice, vanilla extract, ground cinnamon, and ground nutmeg until well combined.
4. Roll Out the Pie Crust:
    - On a lightly floured surface, roll out one disc of chilled pie dough into a circle about 12 inches in diameter. Carefully transfer it to a 9-inch pie dish, gently pressing it into the bottom and up the sides.
5. Fill the Pie:
    - Spoon the strawberry rhubarb filling into the prepared pie crust, spreading it out evenly. Dot the top with small pieces of butter.
6. Top and Seal the Pie:
    - Roll out the second disc of chilled pie dough into a circle about 12 inches in diameter. Place it over the filling.
    - Trim any excess dough from the edges and crimp the edges of the pie crust to seal. Cut a few slits in the top crust to allow steam to escape.
7. Bake the Pie:
    - Brush the top crust with the beaten egg and sprinkle with granulated sugar, if desired.
    - Place the pie on the preheated baking sheet and bake for 45-55 minutes, or until the crust is golden brown and the filling is bubbly.
8. Cool and Serve:
    - Allow the strawberry rhubarb pie to cool on a wire rack for at least 2 hours before serving to allow the filling to set. Serve slices of pie with a scoop of vanilla ice cream or whipped cream, if desired.

Tips:

- If the edges of the pie crust start to brown too quickly during baking, cover them loosely with aluminum foil to prevent burning.
- You can adjust the amount of sugar in the filling according to the sweetness of the strawberries and your personal preference.
- Serve the pie warm or at room temperature for the best flavor and texture.

Enjoy this homemade strawberry rhubarb pie as a delightful dessert that's perfect for spring and summer gatherings!

Maple Brownies

Ingredients:

- 1/2 cup (1 stick) unsalted butter
- 1/2 cup granulated sugar
- 1/2 cup pure maple syrup
- 2 large eggs
- 1 teaspoon vanilla extract
- 1/2 cup all-purpose flour
- 1/3 cup unsweetened cocoa powder
- 1/4 teaspoon salt
- 1/2 cup chopped pecans or walnuts (optional)

Instructions:

1. Preheat the Oven:
    - Preheat your oven to 350°F (175°C). Grease or line an 8x8-inch baking pan with parchment paper.
2. Melt the Butter:
    - In a medium saucepan, melt the butter over medium heat. Remove from heat and let it cool slightly.
3. Mix the Wet Ingredients:
    - In a mixing bowl, whisk together the granulated sugar, maple syrup, eggs, and vanilla extract until well combined.
4. Combine Dry Ingredients:
    - In a separate bowl, sift together the flour, cocoa powder, and salt.
5. Combine Wet and Dry Ingredients:
    - Gradually add the dry ingredients to the wet ingredients, mixing until just combined. Be careful not to overmix.
6. Add Nuts (Optional):
    - Fold in the chopped pecans or walnuts, if using, until evenly distributed in the batter.
7. Bake the Brownies:
    - Pour the batter into the prepared baking pan, spreading it out evenly.
8. Bake:
    - Bake in the preheated oven for 20-25 minutes, or until a toothpick inserted into the center comes out with a few moist crumbs.
9. Cool and Serve:

- Allow the maple brownies to cool in the pan for at least 10-15 minutes before slicing and serving.

Tips:

- Be careful not to overbake the brownies, as they can become dry. It's better to slightly underbake them for a fudgier texture.
- You can adjust the amount of maple syrup according to your taste preferences. If you prefer a stronger maple flavor, you can add more maple syrup or use maple extract in addition to or instead of the syrup.
- For an extra indulgent treat, serve the maple brownies warm with a scoop of vanilla ice cream and a drizzle of maple syrup on top.

Enjoy these delicious homemade maple brownies as a sweet treat with a delightful maple twist!

Butter Cake

Ingredients:

- 1 cup (2 sticks) unsalted butter, softened, plus extra for greasing the pan
- 2 cups all-purpose flour, plus extra for dusting the pan
- 1 1/2 cups granulated sugar
- 4 large eggs, at room temperature
- 1 teaspoon vanilla extract
- 1/2 cup milk, at room temperature
- 1 teaspoon baking powder
- 1/4 teaspoon salt

Instructions:

1. Preheat the Oven:
    - Preheat your oven to 350°F (175°C). Grease and flour a 9-inch round cake pan or line it with parchment paper.
2. Cream the Butter and Sugar:
    - In a large mixing bowl, cream together the softened butter and granulated sugar until light and fluffy, using a hand mixer or stand mixer.
3. Add Eggs and Vanilla:
    - Add the eggs one at a time, beating well after each addition. Then, mix in the vanilla extract until well combined.
4. Combine Dry Ingredients:
    - In a separate bowl, sift together the flour, baking powder, and salt.
5. Alternate Adding Dry Ingredients and Milk:
    - Gradually add the dry ingredients to the butter mixture, alternating with the milk, starting and ending with the dry ingredients. Mix until just combined after each addition, being careful not to overmix.
6. Bake the Cake:
    - Pour the batter into the prepared cake pan and spread it out evenly with a spatula.
    - Bake in the preheated oven for 30-35 minutes, or until a toothpick inserted into the center comes out clean and the top is golden brown.
7. Cool and Serve:
    - Allow the butter cake to cool in the pan for about 10 minutes, then transfer it to a wire rack to cool completely.

- Once cooled, slice and serve the butter cake on its own or with a dusting of powdered sugar, a dollop of whipped cream, or a scoop of ice cream.

Tips:

- Be sure to use softened butter and room temperature eggs and milk for the best results.
- You can customize the flavor of the butter cake by adding lemon zest, almond extract, or other flavorings to the batter.
- To check for doneness, insert a toothpick into the center of the cake. It should come out clean with no wet batter clinging to it.
- Store any leftover butter cake in an airtight container at room temperature for up to 3 days, or in the refrigerator for longer storage.

Enjoy this classic butter cake as a simple yet delicious dessert that's perfect for any occasion!

Peach Cobbler

Ingredients:

For the Peach Filling:

- 6 cups sliced fresh or canned peaches (about 6-8 peaches)
- 1 cup granulated sugar
- 1/4 cup all-purpose flour
- 1 teaspoon ground cinnamon
- 1/4 teaspoon ground nutmeg
- 1 teaspoon vanilla extract
- 2 tablespoons unsalted butter, cut into small pieces

For the Cobbler Topping:

- 1 1/2 cups all-purpose flour
- 1/2 cup granulated sugar
- 2 teaspoons baking powder
- 1/2 teaspoon salt
- 1/2 cup (1 stick) unsalted butter, cold and cut into small pieces
- 1/2 cup milk
- 1 teaspoon vanilla extract

For Assembly:

- Vanilla ice cream or whipped cream (optional, for serving)

Instructions:

1. Preheat the Oven:
   - Preheat your oven to 375°F (190°C).
2. Prepare the Peach Filling:
   - In a large mixing bowl, combine the sliced peaches, granulated sugar, flour, ground cinnamon, ground nutmeg, and vanilla extract. Stir until the peaches are evenly coated.
3. Assemble the Cobbler:
   - Transfer the peach filling to a 9x13-inch baking dish or a similar-sized dish. Dot the top of the filling with the small pieces of butter.
4. Make the Cobbler Topping:

- In a separate mixing bowl, whisk together the flour, sugar, baking powder, and salt.
- Cut in the cold butter using a pastry cutter or your fingers until the mixture resembles coarse crumbs.
- Stir in the milk and vanilla extract until just combined, being careful not to overmix.

5. Add the Topping to the Cobbler:
   - Drop spoonfuls of the cobbler topping evenly over the peach filling in the baking dish.
6. Bake the Cobbler:
   - Place the baking dish in the preheated oven and bake for 40-45 minutes, or until the topping is golden brown and the filling is bubbly.
7. Cool and Serve:
   - Allow the peach cobbler to cool for a few minutes before serving.
   - Serve warm with a scoop of vanilla ice cream or a dollop of whipped cream, if desired.

Tips:

- You can use fresh, canned, or frozen peaches for this recipe. If using canned peaches, be sure to drain them well before using.
- Feel free to adjust the amount of sugar in the filling according to the sweetness of your peaches and your personal preference.
- Leftover peach cobbler can be stored in an airtight container in the refrigerator for up to 3 days. Reheat in the oven or microwave before serving.

Enjoy this homemade peach cobbler as a comforting and delicious dessert that's perfect for summer gatherings and family dinners!

Maple Mousse

Ingredients:

- 1 cup pure maple syrup
- 3 large egg yolks
- 1 tablespoon cornstarch
- 1 1/2 cups heavy cream
- 1 teaspoon vanilla extract
- Optional: whipped cream and maple syrup for garnish

Instructions:

1. Prepare the Maple Syrup Mixture:
    - In a saucepan, heat the maple syrup over medium heat until it comes to a simmer. Reduce the heat to low.
2. Whisk the Egg Yolks:
    - In a heatproof bowl, whisk together the egg yolks and cornstarch until well combined.
3. Temper the Egg Yolks:
    - Slowly pour a small amount of the warm maple syrup into the egg yolk mixture while whisking continuously. This will temper the egg yolks and prevent them from curdling.
4. Combine and Cook:
    - Gradually pour the tempered egg yolk mixture back into the saucepan with the remaining maple syrup, whisking constantly.
    - Cook the mixture over low heat, stirring constantly, until it thickens and coats the back of a spoon, about 5-7 minutes. Do not let it boil.
5. Cool the Mixture:
    - Remove the maple syrup mixture from the heat and let it cool to room temperature. You can speed up the cooling process by placing the saucepan in an ice bath and stirring occasionally.
6. Whip the Heavy Cream:
    - In a separate mixing bowl, whip the heavy cream and vanilla extract until stiff peaks form.
7. Fold in the Maple Mixture:
    - Once the maple syrup mixture has cooled, gently fold it into the whipped cream until well combined. Be careful not to deflate the whipped cream.
8. Chill:

- Transfer the maple mousse to serving glasses or a serving bowl. Cover and refrigerate for at least 2 hours, or until set.
9. Serve:
    - Before serving, garnish the maple mousse with a dollop of whipped cream and a drizzle of maple syrup, if desired.

Tips:

- Make sure to use pure maple syrup for the best flavor.
- Be patient when tempering the egg yolks to avoid scrambling them.
- You can adjust the sweetness of the mousse by adding more or less maple syrup according to your preference.
- Serve the maple mousse chilled for a refreshing and elegant dessert.

Enjoy this light and creamy maple mousse as a delightful ending to any meal!

Maple Bacon Donuts

Ingredients:

For the Donuts:

- 2 cups all-purpose flour
- 1/2 cup granulated sugar
- 2 teaspoons baking powder
- 1/2 teaspoon baking soda
- 1/2 teaspoon salt
- 3/4 cup buttermilk
- 2 large eggs
- 2 tablespoons unsalted butter, melted
- 2 tablespoons pure maple syrup
- 1 teaspoon vanilla extract

For the Maple Glaze:

- 1 cup powdered sugar
- 2 tablespoons pure maple syrup
- 1-2 tablespoons milk or water

For the Topping:

- 6 slices bacon, cooked until crispy and crumbled

Instructions:

1. Preheat the Oven:
    - Preheat your oven to 350°F (175°C). Grease a donut pan with non-stick cooking spray.
2. Prepare the Donut Batter:
    - In a large mixing bowl, whisk together the flour, sugar, baking powder, baking soda, and salt.
    - In a separate bowl, whisk together the buttermilk, eggs, melted butter, maple syrup, and vanilla extract until well combined.
    - Pour the wet ingredients into the dry ingredients and mix until just combined. Be careful not to overmix.
3. Fill the Donut Pan:

- Spoon the batter into a piping bag or a large resealable plastic bag with a corner snipped off. Pipe the batter into the prepared donut pan, filling each cavity about 2/3 full.
4. Bake the Donuts:
    - Place the donut pan in the preheated oven and bake for 10-12 minutes, or until the donuts are lightly golden and spring back when lightly pressed.
5. Cool the Donuts:
    - Remove the donut pan from the oven and let the donuts cool in the pan for a few minutes before transferring them to a wire rack to cool completely.
6. Prepare the Maple Glaze:
    - In a small bowl, whisk together the powdered sugar, maple syrup, and enough milk or water to reach your desired consistency for the glaze.
7. Glaze the Donuts:
    - Dip each cooled donut into the maple glaze, allowing any excess glaze to drip off.
8. Top with Crumbled Bacon:
    - Sprinkle the crumbled bacon over the glazed donuts before the glaze sets.
9. Serve:
    - Allow the glaze to set before serving the maple bacon donuts. Enjoy them fresh or store them in an airtight container for up to 2 days.

Tips:

- Make sure to use real maple syrup for the best flavor in both the donuts and the glaze.
- You can customize the amount of bacon to suit your taste preferences. Some people prefer a light sprinkling, while others like a more generous amount.
- If you don't have a donut pan, you can also bake the batter in a mini muffin tin to make maple bacon donut holes.

Enjoy these indulgent maple bacon donuts as a sweet and savory treat for breakfast or dessert!

Gingerbread Cake

Ingredients:

For the Cake:

- 2 1/4 cups all-purpose flour
- 2 teaspoons ground ginger
- 1 teaspoon ground cinnamon
- 1/4 teaspoon ground cloves
- 1/2 teaspoon baking soda
- 1/2 teaspoon salt
- 3/4 cup unsalted butter, softened
- 3/4 cup packed brown sugar
- 2 large eggs, at room temperature
- 1 cup molasses
- 1 cup hot water

For the Cream Cheese Frosting (optional):

- 8 ounces cream cheese, softened
- 1/2 cup unsalted butter, softened
- 3 cups powdered sugar
- 1 teaspoon vanilla extract

Instructions:

1. Preheat the Oven:
    - Preheat your oven to 350°F (175°C). Grease and flour a 9x13-inch baking pan or two 9-inch round cake pans.
2. Prepare the Dry Ingredients:
    - In a medium bowl, whisk together the flour, ground ginger, ground cinnamon, ground cloves, baking soda, and salt until well combined. Set aside.
3. Cream the Butter and Sugar:
    - In a large mixing bowl, beat the softened butter and brown sugar together until light and fluffy, using a hand mixer or stand mixer.
4. Add Eggs and Molasses:
    - Add the eggs one at a time, beating well after each addition. Then, mix in the molasses until well combined.

5. Combine Wet and Dry Ingredients:
    - Gradually add the dry ingredients to the wet ingredients, alternating with the hot water, beginning and ending with the dry ingredients. Mix until just combined, being careful not to overmix.
6. Bake the Cake:
    - Pour the batter into the prepared baking pan(s) and spread it out evenly.
    - Bake in the preheated oven for 30-35 minutes for a 9x13-inch pan or 25-30 minutes for round cake pans, or until a toothpick inserted into the center comes out clean.
7. Cool the Cake:
    - Allow the cake to cool in the pan(s) for about 10 minutes, then transfer it to a wire rack to cool completely.
8. Prepare the Cream Cheese Frosting (optional):
    - In a mixing bowl, beat the softened cream cheese and butter together until smooth and creamy.
    - Gradually add the powdered sugar and vanilla extract, beating until light and fluffy.
9. Frost the Cake (optional):
    - Once the cake has cooled completely, frost it with the cream cheese frosting, spreading it out evenly over the top and sides of the cake.
10. Serve:
    - Slice and serve the gingerbread cake on its own or with a dollop of whipped cream or a scoop of vanilla ice cream, if desired.

Tips:

- You can adjust the amount of spices in the cake according to your taste preferences. If you prefer a stronger ginger flavor, you can add more ground ginger.
- Make sure to use unsulphured molasses for the best flavor and color in the cake.
- Store any leftover cake in an airtight container at room temperature for up to 3 days, or in the refrigerator for longer storage.

Enjoy this homemade gingerbread cake as a festive and delicious dessert that's perfect for any occasion!

Caramel Apple Pie

Ingredients:

For the Pie Crust:

- 2 1/2 cups all-purpose flour
- 1 teaspoon salt
- 1 tablespoon granulated sugar
- 1 cup unsalted butter, cold and cubed
- 6-8 tablespoons ice water

For the Apple Filling:

- 6-8 large apples (such as Granny Smith or Honeycrisp), peeled, cored, and thinly sliced
- 1/2 cup granulated sugar
- 1/4 cup packed light brown sugar
- 2 tablespoons all-purpose flour
- 1 teaspoon ground cinnamon
- 1/4 teaspoon ground nutmeg
- 1/4 teaspoon salt
- 2 tablespoons lemon juice

For the Caramel Sauce:

- 1 cup granulated sugar
- 6 tablespoons unsalted butter
- 1/2 cup heavy cream
- 1/2 teaspoon salt
- 1 teaspoon vanilla extract

For Assembly:

- Egg wash (1 egg beaten with 1 tablespoon water)
- Coarse sugar, for sprinkling (optional)

Instructions:

1. Prepare the Pie Crust:
    - In a large mixing bowl, whisk together the flour, salt, and granulated sugar.

- Add the cold cubed butter and use a pastry cutter or your fingers to cut the butter into the flour mixture until it resembles coarse crumbs with some pea-sized pieces.
- Gradually add the ice water, a tablespoon at a time, mixing until the dough just begins to come together. Be careful not to overwork the dough.
- Divide the dough into two equal portions, shape each into a disc, wrap in plastic wrap, and refrigerate for at least 1 hour, or until firm.

2. Preheat the Oven:
    - Preheat your oven to 375°F (190°C).
3. Prepare the Apple Filling:
    - In a large mixing bowl, toss together the sliced apples, granulated sugar, brown sugar, flour, cinnamon, nutmeg, salt, and lemon juice until the apples are evenly coated.
4. Make the Caramel Sauce:
    - In a saucepan, heat the granulated sugar over medium heat, stirring constantly with a wooden spoon until it melts and turns amber in color.
    - Add the butter and stir until melted and combined.
    - Slowly pour in the heavy cream while stirring constantly. Be careful, as the mixture will bubble up.
    - Remove the saucepan from the heat and stir in the salt and vanilla extract. Set aside to cool slightly.
5. Roll Out the Pie Crust:
    - On a lightly floured surface, roll out one disc of chilled pie dough into a circle about 12 inches in diameter. Carefully transfer it to a 9-inch pie dish, gently pressing it into the bottom and up the sides.
6. Fill the Pie:
    - Arrange the apple filling in the prepared pie crust, mounding it slightly in the center. Drizzle about 1/4 cup of the caramel sauce over the apples.
7. Top and Seal the Pie:
    - Roll out the second disc of chilled pie dough into a circle about 12 inches in diameter. Place it over the filling.
    - Trim any excess dough from the edges and crimp the edges of the pie crust to seal. Cut a few slits in the top crust to allow steam to escape.
8. Bake the Pie:
    - Brush the top crust with the egg wash and sprinkle with coarse sugar, if desired.
    - Place the pie on a baking sheet to catch any drips and bake in the preheated oven for 45-55 minutes, or until the crust is golden brown and the filling is bubbly.

9. **Cool and Serve:**
    - Allow the caramel apple pie to cool on a wire rack for at least 2 hours before serving.
    - Serve slices of pie with additional caramel sauce drizzled over the top and a scoop of vanilla ice cream, if desired.

Tips:

- You can use store-bought caramel sauce instead of making your own if you prefer.
- Make sure to use firm apples that hold their shape well when baked, such as Granny Smith or Honeycrisp.
- Serve the caramel apple pie warm or at room temperature for the best flavor and texture.

Enjoy this indulgent caramel apple pie as a delicious dessert that's perfect for fall or any time of year!

Maple Custard

Ingredients:

- 2 cups whole milk
- 1/2 cup pure maple syrup
- 4 large eggs
- 1/2 teaspoon vanilla extract
- Pinch of salt
- Ground cinnamon or nutmeg, for garnish (optional)

Instructions:

1. Preheat the Oven:
    - Preheat your oven to 325°F (160°C). Place six ramekins or custard cups in a baking dish large enough to hold them without touching.
2. Heat the Milk and Maple Syrup:
    - In a saucepan, heat the milk and maple syrup over medium heat until it just starts to steam. Do not let it boil.
3. Prepare the Egg Mixture:
    - In a mixing bowl, whisk together the eggs, vanilla extract, and salt until well combined.
4. Temper the Eggs:
    - Slowly pour a small amount of the warm milk mixture into the egg mixture while whisking continuously. This will temper the eggs and prevent them from curdling.
5. Combine the Mixtures:
    - Gradually add the tempered egg mixture back into the saucepan with the remaining milk mixture, whisking constantly until smooth and well combined.
6. Strain the Mixture:
    - Strain the custard mixture through a fine-mesh sieve to remove any lumps or air bubbles.
7. Fill the Ramekins:
    - Pour the custard mixture evenly into the prepared ramekins.
8. Bake the Custard:
    - Carefully pour hot water into the baking dish around the ramekins, creating a water bath that reaches about halfway up the sides of the ramekins.

- Place the baking dish in the preheated oven and bake for 35-40 minutes, or until the custard is set around the edges but still slightly jiggly in the center.
9. Chill and Serve:
    - Remove the ramekins from the water bath and let them cool to room temperature. Then, cover and refrigerate for at least 2 hours, or until chilled and set.
    - Before serving, sprinkle the chilled maple custards with ground cinnamon or nutmeg, if desired.

Tips:

- Make sure not to overbake the custards, as they will continue to set as they cool.
- You can adjust the sweetness of the custard by using more or less maple syrup according to your taste preferences.
- For a richer custard, you can use half-and-half or heavy cream instead of whole milk.
- Serve the maple custards chilled as a delicious and elegant dessert.

Enjoy this creamy and flavorful maple custard as a delightful ending to any meal!

www.ingramcontent.com/pod-product-compliance
Lightning Source LLC
LaVergne TN
LVHW061939070526
838199LV00060B/3887